The

Medical Astrology Series

Volume 1 Planets and Diseases

Dr Apurva Tripathi (Dr Om Shandilya)

manda
Publishers

Title: The Medical Astrology Series Volume 1 Planets and Diseases

Author: Dr Apurva Tripathi (Dr Om Shandilya)

First Published by Manda Publishers in 2026

ISBN: 978-93-6402-615-4
Price in INR: 279/-
Manda Publishers
www.mandapublishers.com
publish@mandapublishers.com
+91 9999190496

Distributed by:
Amazon, Flipkart, Manda Publishers etc.

Printer:
Manipal Technologies

Author's Introduction

Dr. Om Shandilya (Apurva) is a renowned Medical Astrology expert, Astrologer, and Vastu Consultant, with more than 30 years of dedicated research and practice in Vedic Astrology, particularly in the field of planetary influence on human health, disease predisposition, and healing potential.

Holding an M.Sc. from Banaras Hindu University (BHU) and an MBA from Lucknow University, Dr. Om Shandilya further pursued advanced academic research in astrology, earning a Master's degree and PhD in Astrology. His doctoral thesis, *"The Role of Planets in Human Health,"* forms the intellectual foundation of this book. His work bridges classical astrological wisdom with systematic observation of diseases, making Medical Astrology a practical diagnostic, preventive, and supportive discipline rather than a purely theoretical subject.

Dr. Om Shandilya's approach recognizes that true health is multidimensional, influenced not only by planetary forces but also by Ayurvedic constitution (Prakriti), doshic balance (Vata–Pitta–Kapha), lifestyle, diet, mental state, and daily discipline. Accordingly, this book integrates Ayurvedic principles to explain how planetary imbalances manifest through doshic disturbances and organ vulnerability, offering a holistic understanding of disease causation.

In addition, the role of Yoga is emphasized as a preventive and supportive tool for health management. Yogic practices such as asana, pranayama, meditation, and relaxation techniques are viewed as natural methods to strengthen immunity, stabilize the nervous system, improve circulation, and enhance recovery—especially when aligned with planetary periods and individual constitution. Yoga, as presented in this work, is not a cure but a supportive discipline for physical balance, mental clarity, and healing response.

Initiated into astrology during childhood under the guidance of his Nanaji, a revered saint from Azamgarh, Dr. Om Shandilya's method is rooted in spiritual discipline, ethical responsibility, and compassion. Being born and raised in Varanasi, one of the world's oldest centers of spiritual learning, further shaped his deep respect for classical texts, traditional healing sciences, and responsible knowledge transmission.

Parallel to his astrological journey, Dr. Om Shandilya gained substantial professional exposure through his association with Tata Steel–linked industrial organizations, which provided him with an analytical, structured, and data-oriented mindset. This background significantly influenced his case-study-based and evidence-driven approach to Medical Astrology, Ayurveda correlation, and remedial validation.

This book is the outcome of decades of clinical observation, horoscope analysis, planetary correlation with diseases, Ayurvedic doshic mapping, and practical remedial assessment. It aims to provide readers with clear guidelines to identify major illnesses through planetary positions, houses, Rashis, and doshic imbalances, while emphasizing prevention, timing of illness, recovery potential, lifestyle correction, and ethical remedies.

Written for students of astrology, practicing astrologers, Ayurveda learners, yoga practitioners, and health professionals interested in integrative sciences, this book serves as a practical reference manual rather than a speculative narrative.

Through this work, Dr. Om Shandilya seeks to establish Medical Astrology—supported by Ayurveda and Yoga—as a responsible, research-oriented, and humane discipline that complements modern healthcare by offering insight into predisposition, timing, lifestyle alignment, and healing capacity, always guided by accuracy, humility, and human welfare.

Preface

Health has always been the greatest concern of human life. While modern medical science has achieved remarkable progress in diagnosis and treatment, the root predisposition of disease, its timing, recurrence, and an individual's capacity to heal often remain unexplained. Medical Astrology, when studied alongside Ayurveda and Yoga, seeks to address these deeper dimensions by examining the planetary influences, constitutional imbalances, and lifestyle factors that govern the human body, mind, and immunity.

Ancient Vedic texts establish that the human body is a microcosm of the universe, continuously influenced by planetary movements as well as the three doshas—Vata, Pitta, and Kapha. Every planet governs specific organs, tissues, doshic tendencies, and psychological functions. When planetary energies become imbalanced, they often disturb doshic equilibrium, eventually manifesting as illness—sometimes years before physical symptoms appear. Recognizing these early signals through astrology and Ayurveda is one of the greatest strengths of this integrative approach.

Yoga, as described in classical texts, acts as a preventive and supportive discipline, strengthening the nervous system, improving circulation, enhancing immunity, and stabilizing mental health. When practiced in alignment with individual constitution and planetary periods, asana, pranayama, meditation, and relaxation techniques help restore balance and improve the body's healing response. In this context, Yoga is presented not as a cure, but as a supportive science for maintaining physical, mental, and energetic harmony.

This book is the result of over three decades of observation, research, and practical application. It is not based on theoretical assumptions alone, but on systematic horoscope analysis, Ayurvedic doshic mapping, real-life case studies, and correlation of planetary positions with documented health conditions. The objective is to provide clear and structured guidelines to identify disease tendencies, severity, recovery potential, and preventive measures through an integrated astrological, Ayurvedic, and yogic framework.

Special emphasis has been placed on:

- Planet-wise disease patterns and their Ayurvedic doshic associations

- House-wise health indications (especially the 1st, 6th, 8th, and 12th houses)
- Rashi-based bodily mapping (Kaal Purush concept)
- Role of Mahadasha, Antardasha, and transits in disease onset, progression, and recovery
- Preventive astrology, lifestyle correction, and ethical remedial measures
- Supportive role of diet, daily routine (Dinacharya), seasonal care (Ritucharya), and Yoga practices

This book does not intend to replace modern medicine. Instead, it aims to complement medical science by offering insight into predisposition, timing, lifestyle influence, and psychological factors affecting disease and healing. Astrological, Ayurvedic, and yogic insights presented here should always function in support of medical diagnosis and treatment, never as a substitute.

Written for students of astrology, practicing astrologers, Ayurveda learners, yoga practitioners, and health professionals interested in integrative sciences, this book encourages responsible practice, humility, and continuous learning. Medical Astrology, when supported by Ayurveda and Yoga, is a powerful tool—but it must be applied with sensitivity, ethics, and compassion.

If this work helps readers develop a deeper understanding of health, prevent suffering through early awareness, and guide individuals toward timely medical intervention and balanced living, its purpose will be fulfilled.

— Dr. Om Shandilya (Apurva)

Medical & Wellness Disclaimer

This book presents information based on the principles of Vedic Astrology, Medical Astrology, Ayurveda, and Yoga, intended solely for educational and informational purposes. The content is designed to promote awareness of holistic health concepts, lifestyle balance, and preventive wellness approaches. It is not intended to diagnose, treat, cure, or prevent any disease.

Astrology, Ayurveda, and Yoga are complementary and traditional knowledge systems that focus on understanding constitutional tendencies, energetic imbalances, and lifestyle alignment. The interpretations, observations, dietary suggestions, yogic practices, or remedial measures discussed in this book should not be considered a substitute for professional medical advice, diagnosis, or treatment.

Readers are strongly advised to consult qualified medical doctors, licensed healthcare professionals, or registered Ayurvedic practitioners for any medical condition, symptoms, or health concerns. No reader should delay, modify, or discontinue medical treatment or prescribed medication based on information contained in this book.

Any dietary guidance, yogic practices, breathing techniques, or lifestyle recommendations mentioned should be adopted only after considering individual health conditions, age, physical capacity, and medical history, and preferably under professional supervision.

The author does not claim to practice modern medicine. All case references or examples are provided purely for academic understanding and illustrative purposes, and outcomes may vary based on individual constitution (Prakriti), planetary configurations, lifestyle, and adherence to medical advice.

The author and publisher disclaim all responsibility and liability for any direct or indirect consequences arising from the application or interpretation of the content presented herein. All health-related decisions remain the sole responsibility of the reader.

By reading this book, the reader acknowledges and agrees that Astrology, Ayurveda, and Yoga should be practiced ethically, responsibly, and only as supportive systems, working in harmony with modern medical science for overall well-being.

Blessing Message

From Mother – In Loving Memory of Father

Dear Dr. Apurva Tripathi (Dr. Om Shandilya),

It is a matter of great pride, happiness, and emotional satisfaction for me to see the publication of your first book. Your dedication, discipline, and commitment to sharing knowledge for the benefit of society are truly commendable.

Writing is not only an art but also a responsibility and a form of service. From your early years, I have seen in you a deep curiosity, strong determination, and a sincere desire to guide and support others. This book is the result of your hard work, faith, and continuous pursuit of knowledge and excellence.

As a writer myself, I have been blessed to contribute to literature through novels such as "Nagfani" and "Andha Moh", along with several books of stories, poetry, and culinary writings, and poetry recitations on All India Radio. It gives me immense satisfaction to see the literary and intellectual tradition of our family being carried forward by you with such meaningful work.

Today, although your father, Late Shri Prabha Shanker Tripathi, is not physically present with us, his values, guidance, and blessings remain a constant source of strength. He would have been deeply proud to witness this important milestone in your life. May his divine blessings always guide and protect you.

I pray to God that your knowledge and wisdom continue to grow and that your work brings recognition, success, and the opportunity to serve humanity. May your writing inspire, guide, and bring positive transformation to many lives.

With my love and blessings,

Smt. Usha Tripathi

Author of *Nagfani*, *Andha Moh*, and other literary works

(Mother)

In loving memory of

Late Shri Prabha Shanker Tripathi

Medical Astrology Series – Volume 1

Chapter-wise Disease Index (14 Chapter System)

Chapter 1 – Infectious & Fever-Related Diseases

1. Common Cold (Rhinitis)

2. Cough (Kāsa)

3. Fever (Jvara)

4. Measles (Khasra)

5. Chickenpox

Chapter 2 – Blood & Immunity Disorders

6. Leukemia (Blood Cancer)

7. Cancer (General)

8. Fatigue (Chronic Tiredness / Low Energy)

Chapter 3 – Endocrine & Metabolic Disorders

9. Diabetic Retinopathy

Chapter 4 – Cardiovascular Diseases

(Reserved for future cardiovascular diseases)

Chapter 5 – Respiratory Disorders

10. Lung-Related Issues

Chapter 6 – Digestive & Liver Disorders

11. Abdominal Pain (Udar Shoola)

Chapter 14 – Reproductive & Gynecological Disorders

Concept Note

Medical Jyotish ke Vishnu Puranik Adhar

By Dr. Om Shandilya (Apurva)
(Medical Astrologer & Researcher),
Address : B 238, Priyadarshini Vihar,
Delhi-110092 ,
Mob-9278714777 / 9811798030

1. Background

The synthesis of Vedic Jyotish and Ayurvedic wisdom represents one of the most profound aspects of India's spiritual and scientific heritage. In the Vishnu Purana, the cosmic anatomy of the Universe (Vishva Purusha) is described through planetary and elemental correlations that reflect both the macrocosm (cosmos) and microcosm (human body).

This work seeks to decode those ancient relationships through an integrated framework of Medical Astrology, exploring how planetary configurations influence the Tridosha (Vata, Pitta, Kapha) and health constitution.

2. Purpose

To present a systematic and puranic foundation of Medical Jyotish — where planetary lords, nakshatras, and bhava correspondences are studied in relation to:

- Ayurvedic physiology (Dosha–Dhatu–Agni–Srotas system)
- Vishnu Puranic cosmology (Devatā-tattva and Avatāra symbolism)
- Predictive and preventive health astrology

This study aims to bridge classical Jyotish with spiritual health diagnostics, offering both scholarly depth and practical application for students and practitioners.

3. Research Objectives

1. To identify Vishnu Puranic references linking cosmic creation and human physiology.
2. To analyze graha and bhava impacts on disease tendencies via Ayurvedic parameters.
3. To systematize Medical Jyotish as a complementary discipline within Vedic astrology education.
4. To correlate findings with classical texts such as Brihat Parāśara Hora Śāstra, Charaka Samhita, and Vishnu Purana.

4. Methodology

- Textual and comparative study of Puranic, Ayurvedic, and Jyotish sources.
- Case analysis through modern horoscopic data.
- Classification of diseases by Dosha dominance and planetary afflictions.
- Interpretative mapping of Vishnu's Avatāras as healing archetypes within Jyotish framework.

5. Expected Outcomes

- Development of a Puranic-Ayurvedic model of Medical Jyotish.
- Academic paper(s) and articles for publication under ICAS / Bharatiya Vidya Bhavan.
- Educational content suitable for astrology students and health researchers.
- Contribution to revival of authentic Jyotish-Āyurveda-Puranic synergy.

Chapter 1

Infectious & Fever-Related Diseases

1. Common Cold (Rhinitis) – An Integrated Astrological, Ayurvedic & Yogic Perspective

Introduction

The **common cold** is generally considered a minor ailment; however, in many individuals it becomes **frecurrent, prolonged, or seasonal**, causing persistent discomfort and reduced immunity. From an integrative perspective, the common cold is not only the result of viral exposure, but also reflects **weak immunity, doshic imbalance, and adverse planetary influences**.

Medical Astrology, Ayurveda, and Yoga together help in understanding **why certain individuals are more prone to repeated colds**, how planetary periods influence susceptibility, and what preventive and supportive measures can be adopted.

Common Causes of Cold (Medical & Lifestyle Factors)

From a general medical and lifestyle viewpoint, the common cold may be triggered by:

- Consumption of cold food or beverages
- Sudden weather or seasonal changes
- Weak immune system
- Exposure to dust, pollution, or allergens
- Viral infections

While these factors explain the immediate cause, they do not fully clarify **recurrence, delayed recovery, or seasonal vulnerability**, which are better understood through astrology and Ayurveda.

Astrological Causes of Common Cold

According to **Vedic Medical Astrology**, the common cold is primarily associated with disturbances in the **Moon (Chandra)**, along with the influence of **Saturn (Shani)** and **Ketu**.

Key Planetary Indications

- The **Moon** governs immunity, fluids, lungs, and respiratory sensitivity
- **Saturn** contributes to chronicity, weakness, and delayed recovery
- **Ketu** is linked with hidden infections, allergies, and unexplained ailments

Astrological Combinations Indicating Susceptibility

- Moon placed in the **6th, 8th, or 12th house**
- Moon afflicted by **Saturn or Rahu's aspect**
- **Moon–Saturn conjunction**, especially during adverse Dashas
- Afflicted Moon in **Cancer, Virgo, or Pisces**

Such planetary conditions often result in **frequent colds, sinus issues, allergic rhinitis, or weak respiratory immunity**, particularly during Moon- or Saturn-related Dasha and transit periods.

Ayurvedic Perspective on Common Cold

In Ayurveda, the common cold is mainly a **Kapha disorder**, with secondary involvement of **Vata**.

Dosha Involvement

- **Kapha imbalance** causes congestion, mucus accumulation, heaviness, and lethargy
- **Vata imbalance** contributes to dryness, sneezing, irritation, and recurrence

Contributing Ayurvedic Factors

- Weak digestive fire (Mandagni)
- Excessive intake of cold, heavy, or sweet foods

- Irregular routine and inadequate rest
- Suppressed natural urges

Ayurveda emphasizes restoring balance through **diet, warmth, digestion enhancement, and immunity-building measures**.

Yogic Support for Common Cold

Yoga supports recovery by **strengthening immunity, improving respiratory function, and calming the nervous system**.

Recommended Yogic Practices

(To be practiced gently and under guidance)

Pranayama

- Anulom Vilom – balances respiratory flow and immunity
- Bhastrika (mild) – clears nasal congestion
- Kapalbhati (gentle) – improves lung capacity

Asanas

- Tadasana (Mountain Pose)
- Bhujangasana (Cobra Pose)
- Setu Bandhasana (Bridge Pose)

Meditation

- Reduces stress, which weakens immunity
- Supports recovery during unfavorable planetary periods

Yoga acts as a **preventive and supportive practice**, not a replacement for medical care.

Astrological & Spiritual Remedies

Planetary Remedies

1. **Strengthening the Moon**
    - Observe a light fast on Mondays

- Offer raw milk to Lord Shiva

2. **Reducing Rahu–Ketu Influence**
    - Immerse a coconut in flowing water on Wednesday or Saturday

Pacifying Saturn

- Donate mustard oil on Saturdays
- Light a lamp under a Peepal tree

These remedies should be practiced with faith, consistency, and ethical intent.

Home-Based Ayurvedic Remedies

1. **Ginger and Tulsi Tea**
    - Enhances warmth and boosts immunity
2. **Turmeric Milk (Golden Milk)**
    - Reduces inflammation and supports infection recovery
3. **Steam Inhalation**
    - Relieves nasal and throat congestion
4. **Lemon and Honey**
    - Soothes sore throat and reduces bacterial load

Preventive Guidelines

- Avoid cold and heavy foods during seasonal changes
- Maintain regular sleep and daily routine
- Protect the body from cold exposure
- Observe preventive care during adverse Moon or Saturn periods

Ethical Note

The remedies and practices mentioned here are **supportive in nature** and should always complement, not replace, professional medical diagnosis and treatment.

Chapter Insight

Recurring common cold reflects a **combination of weak immunity, Kapha imbalance, and adverse lunar or Saturnine influences**. An integrated approach using **Astrology, Ayurveda, and Yoga** provides effective preventive care and long-term balance.

2. Cough (Kāsa) – An Ayurvedic, Astrological & Yogic Perspective

Introduction

In Ayurveda, **cough (Kāsa)** is primarily considered a **Kapha-dominant disorder**, often involving secondary disturbance of **Vata**. While acute cough may resolve with routine care, a cough that becomes **chronic, recurrent, or seasonal** often indicates deeper imbalances. These may not be limited to physical causes alone but can also arise due to **planetary afflictions, weakened immunity, and lifestyle misalignment**.

Medical Astrology, when studied alongside **Ayurveda and Yoga**, helps explain why certain individuals suffer from **persistent or unexplained cough**, especially during specific planetary periods.

Common Causes of Cough

(Ayurvedic & Medical Perspective)**

From an Ayurvedic and general medical standpoint, cough may arise due to:

- Throat infections (viral or bacterial)
- Exposure to dust, pollution, or allergens
- Excessive intake of cold or refrigerated foods
- Smoking or exposure to strong odors and chemicals
- Respiratory conditions such as asthma or bronchitis

While these causes explain the immediate manifestation, **repetition, chronicity, or delayed healing** often point toward underlying **Kapha imbalance and astrological influence**.

Astrological Causes of Cough

According to **Vedic Medical Astrology**, cough is mainly associated with the affliction of **Mars, Saturn, Ketu, and the Moon**, particularly in relation to the lungs, throat, and respiratory system.

Planetary Associations

- **Mars (Mangal)**
    - Governs inflammation and acute conditions
    - When placed in the **8th or 12th house**, it may cause:
        - Lung inflammation
        - Painful or forceful coughing
        - Respiratory infections
- **Ketu**
    - Indicates hidden, chronic, or difficult-to-diagnose conditions
    - Placement in the **3rd, 6th, or 8th house** may lead to:
        - Persistent or unexplained cough
        - Allergic or dry cough
- **Saturn and Rahu**
    - Associated with chronicity and obstruction
    - Their influence often results in:
        - Long-lasting dry cough
        - Delayed recovery
- **Moon (Chandra)**
    - Governs fluids, immunity, and sensitivity
    - A weak or afflicted Moon can cause:
        - Frequent throat infections
        - Recurring cough due to low immunity

Such conditions often worsen during **adverse Mahadasha, Antardasha, or transit periods** related to these planets.

Ayurvedic Perspective on Cough

In Ayurveda, cough is mainly classified as:

- **Kapha-dominant cough** – mucus, heaviness, congestion
- **Vata-dominant cough** – dryness, irritation, repeated bouts
- **Vata-Kapha combined cough** – chronic and recurrent

Key Ayurvedic Causes

- Weak digestive fire (Mandagni)
- Accumulation of Kapha in chest and throat
- Cold, heavy, or incompatible food intake
- Suppression of natural urges
- Mental stress affecting immunity

Ayurveda emphasizes **clearing Kapha, strengthening digestion, and restoring respiratory balance**.

5. Yogic Support for Cough

Yoga supports respiratory health by **improving lung capacity, clearing airways, and calming the nervous system**.

Recommended Yogic Practices

(To be practiced gently and under guidance)

Pranayama

- Anulom Vilom – balances respiratory flow
- Bhastrika (mild) – clears congestion
- Kapalbhati (gentle) – improves lung strength

Asanas

- Bhujangasana (Cobra Pose)
- Setu Bandhasana (Bridge Pose)
- Tadasana (Mountain Pose)

Meditation

- Reduces stress-induced immune weakness

- Supports recovery during challenging planetary phases

Yoga should always be practiced as a **supportive and preventive discipline**, not as a substitute for medical treatment.

Astrological Remedies for Cough

Mars Remedies

- Offer **jaggery and chickpeas** to Lord Hanuman on Tuesdays
- Chant **"Om Kraam Kreem Kraum Sah Bhaumaya Namah"** 108 times

Ketu Remedies

- Donate **black sesame seeds** on Saturdays
- Feed bread to dogs
- Chant **"Om Kem Ketave Namah"**

Saturn Remedies

- Light a **mustard oil lamp under a Peepal tree** on Saturdays
- Chant **"Om Sham Shanaishcharaya Namah"**

These remedies should be practiced with discipline, faith, and ethical intent.

Ayurvedic & Home Remedies

1. **Honey and Ginger Juice**
    - Mix fresh ginger juice with honey and consume 2–3 times daily
2. **Licorice (Mulethi)**
    - Chew directly or consume powder with warm water to soothe the throat
3. **Tulsi and Black Pepper Decoction**
    - Boil 4–5 tulsi leaves, 2 black peppercorns, ginger, and a little jaggery

4. **Steam Inhalation**
    - Helps clear nasal and throat congestion, especially at night

Preventive Guidelines

- Avoid cold, heavy, and mucus-forming foods
- Protect the throat from cold air and pollution
- Maintain digestive strength
- Observe preventive care during adverse planetary periods

Ethical Note

The information and remedies provided here are **supportive and preventive in nature**. They should always be used **alongside professional medical diagnosis and treatment**, not as a replacement.

Chapter Insight

Chronic or recurring cough reflects a **Kapha imbalance combined with planetary affliction**, particularly involving **Mars, Saturn, Ketu, and the Moon**. An integrated approach using **Medical Astrology, Ayurveda, and Yoga** helps in understanding susceptibility, reducing recurrence, and restoring long-term respiratory balance.

3. Fever (Jvara) – An Integrated Ayurvedic, Astrological & Yogic Analysis

Introduction

Fever (**Jvara**) is one of the body's most fundamental defense mechanisms. It represents a **systemic response to infection, inflammation, or internal imbalance**. From a medical standpoint, fever signals that the immune system is actively fighting a disturbance. However, Ayurveda and Medical Astrology go deeper by explaining **why fever arises in a particular individual, why it recurs, and why recovery may be delayed**.

In Ayurveda, fever is considered a disorder involving **imbalance of Vata, Pitta, and Kapha**, with **Pitta** playing a dominant role due to its association with heat and metabolism. Vedic Medical Astrology further explains fever through **planetary afflictions**, especially those involving fiery and obstructive planets.

Common Causes of Fever

(Medical Perspective)**

From a modern medical viewpoint, fever may occur due to:

- Viral and bacterial infections (such as viral fever, influenza, typhoid)
- Inflammation or internal infection
- Weak or compromised immune system
- Excessive exposure to heat or environmental stress
- Allergies, psychological stress, or lack of proper sleep

While these causes explain the immediate trigger, they do not always explain **timing, recurrence, or severity**, which is where astrology and Ayurveda provide deeper insight.

Ayurvedic Understanding of Fever (Jvara)

Ayurveda describes fever as a result of:

- Disturbance in **Agni (digestive fire)**
- Accumulation of toxins (**Ama**)
- Imbalance of **doshas**, especially Pitta

Dosha-wise Fever Patterns

- **Pitta-dominant fever**: High temperature, thirst, inflammation
- **Vata-dominant fever**: Chills, body pain, irregular fever pattern
- **Kapha-dominant fever**: Mild fever with heaviness and lethargy

According to Ayurveda, improper diet, weak digestion, stress, and seasonal changes weaken immunity and allow fever to manifest.

Astrological Causes of Fever

In **Vedic Medical Astrology**, fever is strongly associated with **Mars, Saturn, Rahu, Ketu, and the Moon**. Affliction of these planets creates internal imbalance, excessive heat, or obstruction in bodily systems.

Planetary Influences

Mars (Mangal)

- Represents fire, heat, inflammation, and infections
- If weak or afflicted in the **4th or 6th house**, it may cause:
    - Acute fever
    - Inflammatory conditions
    - Recurrent infections

Saturn (Shani) and Rahu

- Represent chronicity, obstruction, and toxicity
- Placement in the **8th or 12th house** may result in:
    - Long-lasting or unexplained fever

- Slow recovery
- Fever during stressful or debilitated health phases

Ketu

- Causes hidden or mysterious illnesses
- When placed in the **8th or 12th house**, it may lead to:
  - Sudden fever
  - Fever with unclear diagnosis
  - Recurrent infections

Moon (Chandra)

- Governs immunity, fluids, and emotional balance
- A weak or afflicted Moon can disturb body temperature regulation, leading to:
  - Recurrent fever
  - Fever triggered by stress or emotional instability

Fever often appears or intensifies during **specific Mahadasha, Antardasha, or adverse planetary transits** related to these planets.

Yogic Support in Fever Management

Yoga supports recovery by **stabilizing metabolism, calming the nervous system, and improving immunity**. During fever, strenuous practices should be avoided.

Recommended Yogic Practices

(Only after temperature subsides and under guidance)

Pranayama

- Anulom Vilom – balances heat and oxygen flow
- Sheetali / Sheetkari – cooling pranayama for excess Pitta

Meditation

- Reduces stress-induced fever
- Enhances immune response

Yoga should be practiced **only as supportive care**, never during acute high fever.

Astrological Remedies for Fever

Mars Affliction Remedies

- Observe a **fast on Tuesdays**
- Offer **sesame seeds, jaggery, and chickpeas** to Lord Hanuman
- Chant **"Om Kraam Kreem Kraum Sah Bhaumaya Namah"**

Saturn and Rahu Remedies

- Light a **mustard oil lamp under a Peepal tree** on Saturdays
- Offer sesame seeds
- Chant **"Om Sham Shanaishcharaya Namah"**
- For Rahu, immerse a coconut in flowing water

Ketu Remedies

- Donate **black sesame seeds** on Saturdays
- Feed bread to black dogs
- Chant **"Om Kem Ketave Namah"**

These remedies help reduce planetary imbalance and support recovery when practiced with discipline and sincerity.

Ayurvedic & Home Remedies for Fever

1. **Tulsi Decoction**
    - Boil tulsi leaves with ginger and cloves
    - Helps regulate body temperature and boost immunity

2. **Lemon and Honey Water**
    - Mix lemon juice and honey in lukewarm water
    - Maintains hydration and reduces fever discomfort
3. **Turmeric Milk**
    - Consume warm turmeric milk at night
    - Reduces inflammation and strengthens immunity
4. **Adequate Hydration**
    - Drink sufficient water to eliminate excess heat and toxins
5. **Cold Compress / Ice Pack**
    - Apply gently when body temperature is excessively high

Preventive Guidelines

- Maintain strong digestion and balanced diet
- Avoid excessive heat-producing foods during Pitta aggravation
- Manage stress and ensure proper rest
- Take extra care during adverse planetary periods

Ethical & Medical Disclaimer

Astrological, Ayurvedic, and Yogic remedies discussed in this chapter are **supportive and preventive in nature**. They must always be practiced **alongside professional medical diagnosis and treatment**, never as a replacement.

Chapter Insight

Fever reflects an **internal imbalance of doshas combined with planetary afflictions**, especially involving **Mars, Saturn, Rahu, Ketu, and the Moon**. An integrated approach using **Medical Astrology, Ayurveda, and Yoga** provides deeper understanding of susceptibility, timing, and recovery potential.

4. Measles (Khasra)– An Integrated Astrological, Ayurvedic & Yogic Perspective

Introduction

Measles is a **highly contagious viral disease**, most commonly affecting children. Along with medical prevention and care, **astrology provides insight into susceptibility, immunity, and recovery patterns**, especially in childhood illnesses.

What is Measles (Khasra)?

- Measles is a **viral infection**, more common in children.
- It spreads easily through air and contact.
- Common symptoms include:
    - High fever
    - Cough and runny nose
    - Red, watery, and irritated eyes
    - Red rashes spreading over the body
- Measles can be **effectively prevented by vaccination** (MMR vaccine).

Medical Perspective (Brief)

- Caused by the **Measles virus**
- Weak immunity increases susceptibility
- Complications may include pneumonia, ear infections, or weakness if untreated
- Proper rest, hydration, and medical supervision are essential

Astrological Perspective on Measles

In **Vedic Astrology**, certain planets and houses are associated with **immunity, skin disorders, infections, and childhood diseases**.

Key Planets Associated with Measles:

- **Rahu & Ketu** – Sudden infections, skin eruptions, viral diseases
- **Saturn (Shani)** – Prolonged illness, weakness, delayed recovery
- **Moon (Chandra)** – Immunity, fluids, and resistance power
- **Mercury (Budh)** – Nervous system and childhood health

Key Houses:

- **6th House** – Diseases and infections
- **8th House** – Sudden illness and complications

Astrological Indications:

- Rahu or Ketu placed in or afflicting the **6th house**
- Weak Moon or Mercury in the birth chart
- Malefic influence on Moon during early childhood
- Such combinations may increase vulnerability to **viral fevers, rashes, and skin-related infections**

Astrological Remedies (Supportive)

These remedies are supportive in nature and should always accompany proper medical care.

General Remedies:

- **Rahu Mantra**:
  "Om Raam Rahave Namah" – 108 times
- **Ketu Mantra**:
  "Om Kem Ketave Namah" – 108 times
  (Best chanted on Tuesday or Saturday)

Saturn Remedies:

- Donate **black sesame seeds, mustard oil, or iron items** on Saturdays
- Offer mustard oil to Lord Shani

Immunity-Strengthening Mantras:

- **Gayatri Mantra**
- **Mahamrityunjaya Mantra**
  (Believed to enhance protection and recovery)

Ayurvedic & Home Remedies

(If Measles Occurs)

- Bathing with **Neem leaves water** helps soothe skin and rashes
- Light, easily digestible food
- Fresh fruits and adequate fluids
- Complete rest and isolation to prevent spread

Chapter Insight

Measles is primarily a **viral and preventable disease**, but from an astrological viewpoint, **Rahu–Ketu influence, weak Moon, and afflicted 6th house** indicate vulnerability to such infections. While **vaccination and medical care are essential**, astrological remedies, mantras, and Ayurvedic practices can support **immunity, faster recovery, and overall resilience**.

5. Chickenpox– An Integrated Astrological, Ayurvedic & Yogic Perspective

Introduction

Chickenpox is a **viral infection caused by the Varicella-Zoster Virus (VZV)**. It commonly affects children but can also occur in adults, often with greater severity. While medical treatment is primary and essential, **astrology and traditional remedies are sometimes used as supportive approaches** for immunity and recovery.

Chickenpox – Brief Overview

- **Symptoms**:
  - Red, itchy rashes and blisters
  - Fever
  - Fatigue and weakness
  - Headache
- **Mode of Transmission**:
  - Highly contagious
  - Spreads through **airborne droplets** or **direct contact** with blisters/rashes
- **Treatment**:
  - Doctor-prescribed antiviral medicines
  - Fever-control medications
  - Anti-itching and skin-soothing measures

Medical Perspective

Primary Medical Causes:

1. **Viral Infection**
   - Chickenpox is caused by the **Varicella-Zoster Virus**.
   - The virus spreads rapidly through air or close physical contact.

2. **Weak Immune System**
    - Children, pregnant women, elderly individuals, or those on immunosuppressive medication are more vulnerable.
3. **First-Time Infection**
    - Initial exposure to the virus causes Chickenpox.
    - The virus may remain dormant in the body and can later reactivate as **Herpes Zoster (Shingles)**.

Astrological Perspective

In **Vedic Astrology**, skin diseases, viral infections, and childhood illnesses are linked to specific planets and houses.

Key Planets Involved:

- **Ketu** – Skin eruptions, sudden diseases
- **Rahu** – Viral infections, contagious disorders
- **Saturn (Shani)** – Weak immunity, delayed recovery
- **Moon (Chandra)** – Immunity, body fluids, resistance power

Key House:

- **6th House** – House of disease and infection

Astrological Indications:

- Rahu or Ketu influencing the **6th house**
- Weak Moon or Saturn in the birth chart
- Such combinations may indicate susceptibility to **skin rashes, viral fevers, and contagious diseases**

Astrological Remedies (Supportive)

These remedies are complementary and should never replace medical treatment.

Rahu–Ketu Remedies:

- **Ketu Mantra**:
  "Om Ketave Namah" – 108 times daily

- **Rahu Mantra**:
  "Om Rahave Namah" – 108 times daily

Saturn Remedies:

- Light a **mustard oil lamp on Saturdays**
- Recite **Hanuman Chalisa** regularly

Home & Ayurvedic Remedies

(During Chickenpox)

- **Neem Leaves**:
  - Add Neem leaves to bath water
  - Keep Neem leaves in the patient's room to help prevent infection spread
- **Oatmeal Bath**:
  - Reduces itching and skin irritation
- **Turmeric & Sandalwood Paste**:
  - Apply gently on rashes to reduce burning and itching
- **Tulsi Decoction**:
  - Helps boost immunity and reduce fever

Precautions

- Keep the infected person **isolated** to prevent transmission
- Do **not scratch** blisters to avoid scars and secondary infection
- Ensure **adequate fluids, light diet, and complete rest**

Chapter Insight

Chickenpox is a **highly contagious but manageable viral disease.** From an astrological standpoint, **Rahu–Ketu influence, weak Moon, and afflicted 6th house** may indicate vulnerability to such infections. **Medical care and vaccination are essential**, while astrology, Ayurveda, and home remedies can provide **supportive relief, immunity enhancement, and smoother recovery**.

Chapter 2

Blood & Immunity Disorders

6. Leukemia (Blood Cancer) – An Integrated Astrological, Ayurvedic & Yogic Perspective

(Medical care is essential. Astrology provides emotional, karmic, and spiritual support only — not a cure.)

Medical Perspective

Symptoms:

- Persistent fatigue and weakness
- Frequent infections (low immunity)
- Easy bruising or excessive bleeding
- Bone or joint pain
- Fever, night sweats
- Swollen lymph nodes, liver, or spleen
- Unexplained weight loss

Primary Causes:

- Genetic mutations in blood-forming cells
- Bone marrow dysfunction
- Radiation or chemical exposure
- Weak immune system
- Viral or environmental triggers (in some cases)

Astrological Perspective

Leukemia relates to **blood, bone marrow, immunity, and karmic affliction**, making it one of the most complex diseases astrologically.

Key Planets & Houses:

Important Houses:

- **1st House (Lagna):** Overall health, immunity, vitality
- **6th House:** Disease and illness
- **8th House:** Chronic, hidden, or life-threatening disease
- **12th House:** Hospitalization, isolation, energy loss
- **2nd & 7th Houses (Maraka):** Life-threatening potential (only with strong affliction)

Key Planets:

- **Mars:** Blood, bone marrow, vitality
- **Moon:** Body fluids, immunity, emotional strength
- **Sun:** Bone marrow, life force
- **Saturn:** Chronic suffering, degeneration
- **Rahu / Ketu:** Karmic, toxic, hidden diseases

Astrological Combinations Indicating Susceptibility:

- Severely afflicted **Mars** (with Saturn / Rahu / Ketu) in health-related houses
- Malefic dominance in **6th, 8th, or 12th house**
- **Rahu or Ketu in Lagna** without benefic aspects
- **Debilitated Moon or Sun**, especially in 6th/8th/12th house
- Onset during **Dasha / Antardasha** of afflicted Mars, Rahu, or Saturn

Astrological Remedies

(Supportive and spiritual in nature; never a substitute for medical treatment)

Mantras & Chanting:

- **Mahamrityunjaya Mantra** – For life force, protection, and healing:

Om Tryambakam Yajamahe
Sugandhim Pushtivardhanam
Urvarukamiva Bandhanan
Mrityor Mukshiya Maamritat → Chant **108 times daily**

• **Mars Mantra** – For blood strength and vitality:
"Om Bhaumaya Namah"
→ Chant **108 times on Tuesdays**

Gemstone Remedies

(Only after proper horoscope analysis)

• **Red Coral** – If Mars is benefic and supportive
• **Pearl** – If Moon is weak (for immunity and emotional balance)
• If chart is heavily afflicted → **Avoid gemstones**, prefer mantras and charity

Yogic & Ayurvedic Support

• Gentle **pranayama** (only with medical approval)
• Meditation for mental resilience
• Ayurvedic support strictly as **complementary care**

Dietary Recommendations:

• Light, easily digestible, immunity-supportive diet
• Fresh fruits, vegetables, adequate hydration
• Avoid toxins, alcohol, and processed foods

Charity & Healing Acts (Seva):

• Support **blood donation drives** or leukemia foundations
• Donate **red lentils (masoor dal)** or **jaggery** on Tuesdays
• Help children's cancer wards or medical aid institutions

Chapter Insight:

• Leukemia reflects **deep karmic patterns affecting blood, immunity, and vitality**
• Mars–Moon–Sun affliction is central in disease manifestation
• Astrology aids in **timing, mental strength, and spiritual resilience**, while medicine treats the body
• Healing is strongest when **medical science + inner strength + spiritual balance** work together

7. Cancer– An Integrated Astrological, Ayurvedic & Yogic Perspective

Introduction

Cancer is a **serious disease** in which the body's cells begin to grow **uncontrollably**. These abnormal cells can invade surrounding tissues and may spread to other parts of the body (metastasis). Cancer exists in many forms, such as **breast cancer, blood cancer (leukemia), lung cancer**, and others. Its causes may include **genetic factors, lifestyle habits, environmental exposure, and prolonged stress**.

Medical Reasons of Cancer

Cancer does not develop due to a single cause. It is usually the result of **multiple biological, genetic, and environmental factors** acting together.

Gene Mutations (Changes in DNA)

- The primary cause of cancer is **mutation in DNA.**
- These mutations affect genes that regulate **cell growth, division, and cell death**.
- When these control mechanisms fail, cells continue to multiply without restraint.

Viral Infections

Certain long-term infections can increase cancer risk:

- **HPV (Human Papillomavirus)** → Cervical cancer
- **Hepatitis B & C** → Liver cancer
- **Epstein–Barr Virus (EBV)** → Lymphoma
- **HIV** → Increases risk of multiple cancers due to immune suppression

Smoking and Tobacco Use

- Tobacco contains **carcinogenic chemicals** that damage DNA.

- Increases the risk of cancers of the **lungs, mouth, throat, and urinary bladder**.

Unhealthy Lifestyle

- Excessive junk food intake
- Alcohol consumption
- Obesity
- Physical inactivity
- Chronic mental stress
  These significantly raise cancer risk.

Environmental Factors

- **Radiation exposure**
- **Chemical exposure** (asbestos, benzene, industrial pollutants)
- **UV rays** from excessive sun exposure (skin cancer)

Hereditary / Genetic Predisposition

Some cancers run in families due to inherited gene mutations:

- **BRCA1 / BRCA2** → Breast & ovarian cancer
- **TP53 mutation** → Increased risk of multiple cancers

Common Symptoms of Cancer

- Unusual lumps or swelling in the body
- Sudden or unexplained weight loss
- Persistent fatigue, weakness, or fever
- Abnormal skin changes or sores
- Persistent cough, bleeding, or changes in bowel or urinary habits

Cancer from an Astrological Perspective

In **Vedic Astrology**, certain planets and houses indicate **chronic, serious, or long-lasting diseases**.

Key Planets:

- **Saturn (Shani)** – Chronic, long-term illnesses
- **Rahu & Ketu** – Sudden, mysterious, and severe diseases
- **Moon (Chandra)** – Mental strength and immune balance

Key Houses:

- **6th House** – Disease and health struggles
- **8th House** – Chronic illness, transformation, longevity
- **12th House** – Hospitalization, isolation, medical expenses

Indicative Astrological Combinations:

- Rahu–Ketu placed in or influencing the **6th house**
- Saturn influencing the **8th house**
- Weak or afflicted Moon
- Malefic influence on health-related houses may indicate **complex or long-duration diseases**

Astrological Remedies

(Complementary, not a replacement for medical treatment)

General Remedies:

1. **Rahu–Ketu Shanti Puja**
    - Recommended if Rahu–Ketu are severely afflicted in the horoscope
2. **Hanuman Chalisa Recitation**
    - Regularly on **Tuesdays and Saturdays**
3. **Gemstone Remedies**
    - **Blue Sapphire (Neelam)** for Saturn

- **Hessonite (Gomed)** for Rahu
  Only after proper horoscope analysis

4. **Mahamrityunjaya Mantra**
   - Powerful for healing and mental strength:

Om Tryambakam Yajamahe Sugandhim Pushtivardhanam
Urvarukamiva Bandhanan Mrityor Mukshiya Maamritat

5. **Charity and Service**
   - Cow service, water donation, and helping patients
   - Provides mental relief and positive karmic support

Other Supportive Approaches

- **Yoga and Pranayama** – Helpful in improving stamina and recovery
- **Meditation** – Reduces mental stress and fear
- **Ayurveda & Homeopathy** – Can be used as supportive therapies in some cases (under expert guidance)

Chapter Insight

Cancer is a **multifactorial disease**, arising from genetic mutations, lifestyle habits, environmental exposure, and immune imbalance. From an astrological viewpoint, **Saturn, Rahu, Ketu, and afflicted health-related houses** may indicate susceptibility to chronic or serious illness. While **medical diagnosis and treatment are essential**, astrology, yoga, meditation, and traditional therapies can serve as **supportive tools** for mental strength, resilience, and holistic well-being.

8. Fatigue (Chronic Tiredness, Low Energy, Exhaustion) – An Integrated Astrological, Ayurvedic & Yogic Perspective

Introduction

Fatigue is not only a physical condition but can also arise from **mental, emotional, and spiritual imbalances**. In astrology, certain planets, houses, and combinations are strongly associated with **persistent tiredness, low vitality, and lack of motivation**, even when no major medical cause is evident.

Medical & Holistic Understanding

Fatigue may manifest as:

- Constant tiredness despite adequate rest
- Lack of physical stamina
- Mental heaviness or brain fog
- Low motivation and enthusiasm
- Emotional exhaustion
- Disturbed sleep cycle

Common medical contributors include anemia, hormonal imbalance, stress, poor nutrition, sleep disorders, and chronic illnesses. When medical reports are normal, **astrological factors often provide deeper insight**.

Astrological Perspective on Fatigue

Key Astrological Causes of Fatigue:

1. **Weak or Afflicted Moon (Moon)**
    - Causes mental fatigue, emotional instability, anxiety
    - Leads to disturbed sleep and lack of mental peace
2. **Afflicted Saturn (Saturn)**
    - Results in physical exhaustion, slow recovery

- Excessive hard work with limited results
- Chronic tiredness and heaviness in the body

3. **Rahu–Ketu Influence**
    - Mental confusion, directionless feeling
    - Inner restlessness and psychological drain
    - Sudden energy drops without clear cause
4. **Affliction of the 6th or 12th House**
    - 6th House: chronic illness, weakness, fatigue
    - 12th House: sleep disorders, energy leakage, isolation
    - Leads to long-term or recurring fatigue patterns

Astrological Remedies for Fatigue

Remedies to Strengthen the Moon:

- Wear white clothes on Mondays
- Donate rice, milk, and sugar on Mondays
- Spend a few minutes under moonlight at night
- Chant:
  "Om Cham Chandraya Namah" – 108 times

Remedies to Pacify Saturn:

- Donate black sesame seeds, mustard oil, or black clothes on Saturdays
- Worship the Peepal tree and offer water
- Chant:
  "Om Sham Shanicharaya Namah" – 108 times

Remedies for Rahu–Ketu Imbalance:

- For Rahu:
    - Offer a coconut in flowing water

- Chant: **"Om Raam Rahave Namah"**

- For Ketu:
    - Feed stray dogs with bread
    - Chant: **"Om Kem Ketave Namah"**

General Energy-Enhancing Remedies:

- Practice **Surya Namaskar** daily
- Offer water to the Sun every morning using a copper vessel
- Chant on Sundays:
  "Om Suryaya Namah"
- Follow a light, sattvic diet
- Maintain proper sleep (7–8 hours)

Yogic & Lifestyle Support:

- Pranayama: Anulom–Vilom, Bhramari
- Meditation for mental relaxation
- Early bedtime, reduced screen exposure at night
- Regular sunlight exposure in the morning

Chapter Insight:

Fatigue is often a **signal of planetary imbalance rather than mere physical weakness**. A weak Moon drains the mind, Saturn burdens the body, and Rahu–Ketu disturb inner balance. Strengthening the Moon, pacifying Saturn, and grounding Rahu–Ketu—along with disciplined lifestyle practices—can restore **vitality, clarity, and sustained energy**

Chapter 3

Endocrine & Metabolic Disorders

9. Diabetic Retinopathy – An Integrated Astrological, Ayurvedic & Yogic Perspective

Introduction

Diabetic Retinopathy is a serious eye disorder caused by prolonged diabetes. The retinal blood vessels are damaged, leading to blurred vision, floaters, or, in severe cases, blindness. An integrated approach combining **Medical, Astrological, Ayurvedic, and Yogic insights** helps in understanding susceptibility, preventive measures, and supportive remedies.

Medical Causes of Diabetic Retinopathy

Primary Causes:

- Long-standing uncontrolled blood sugar (Hyperglycemia)
- High blood pressure
- Imbalanced cholesterol and lipid levels

Symptoms:

- Blurred vision
- Floaters or spots in vision
- Difficulty distinguishing colors
- Poor night vision
- Sudden vision loss in severe cases

Types:

- **Non-Proliferative Diabetic Retinopathy (NPDR):** Early stage; bleeding and swelling in retinal vessels
- **Proliferative Diabetic Retinopathy (PDR):** Formation of new abnormal blood vessels causing greater damage

Treatment:

- Strict blood sugar control is essential
- Laser treatment for retinal repair
- Anti-VEGF injections
- Retinal surgery in advanced cases

Astrological Perspective

Key Planets & Houses:

- **Venus (Shukra):** Governs blood and eyes
- **Sun (Surya):** Represents vision and ocular strength
- **Ketu:** Linked to darkness, visual distortions, and shadow effects
- **Saturn (Shani):** Associated with chronic diseases and diabetes
- **6th House:** Disease house
- **12th House:** Related to eye pain, left eye, and vision-related struggles

Astrological Combinations Indicating Susceptibility:

- Venus or Sun afflicted by malefics like Saturn or Ketu
- Malefic influence on the 12th house
- Conjunctions or aspects involving Sun, Venus, Saturn, or Ketu

Astrological Remedies

Sun Remedies:

- Offer water to the Sun every morning

- Chant: Om Ghr̥ṇi Sūryāya Namah – 108 times

Venus Remedies:

- On Fridays, donate curd, white sweets, or silver
- Chant: Om Draam Dreem Draum Sah Shukraya Namah – 108 times

Ketu Remedies:

- Chant: Om Kem Ketave Namah– 108 times
- Feed a black dog
- Immerse a coconut in flowing water on Saturday or Tuesday

Saturn Remedies:

- Light a mustard oil lamp under a Peepal tree on Saturday
- Chant: Om Sham Shanaiścharāya Namah – 108 times

Gemstone Remedies

- **Venus weak:** Diamond or Opal
- **Sun weak:** Ruby (Manikya)
- **Ketu weak:** Hessonite (Gomed)

Gemstones must be chosen only after proper horoscope analysis.

Yogic & Ayurvedic Support

Yogic Practices:

- Trataka meditation – improves concentration and vision
- Anulom-Vilom and Kapalbhati – purifies the body and supports ocular health

Ayurvedic Support:

- Triphala powder – for eye cleansing and vision support
- Jamun seed powder – helps control blood sugar

- Rosewater and cucumber compress – cooling and soothing for eyes

Chapter Insight

Diabetic Retinopathy occurs due to **long-standing diabetes, retinal blood vessel damage, and planetary influences** (Venus, Sun, Saturn, Ketu). A combined approach using **Astrology, Ayurveda, and Yoga** strengthens vision, slows progression, and supports long-term eye health.

Chapter 4

Cardiovascular Diseases

(Reserved for future cardiovascular diseases)

Chapter 5

Respiratory Disorders

10. Lung-Related Issues– An Integrated Astrological, Ayurvedic & Yogic Perspective

Introduction

In **Vedic Astrology**, the lungs are primarily governed by the **Gemini zodiac sign**, ruled by **Mercury**, and are closely connected with the **Third House** of the natal chart. Lung health is also influenced by emotional balance, environmental factors, and chronic planetary afflictions.

Key Planets & Houses

- **Mercury**
  Governs the respiratory system, lungs, nervous coordination, and breathing rhythm.
- **Moon**
  Represents bodily fluids, emotional stability, and psychological factors affecting breathing.
- **Saturn**
  Indicates chronic, long-term respiratory conditions when afflicting lung-related planets or houses.
- **Rahu (North Node)**
  Linked with pollution, toxins, smoke, allergies, and unexplained or sudden respiratory disorders.
- **4th House**
  Directly represents the chest, lungs, and heart region.
- **3rd House**
  Associated with breathing capacity and lung strength.

- **6th House**
  Represents disease, infections, and chronic health struggles.

Risky Astrological Combinations (Yogas)

- **Saturn + Rahu conjunction** in Gemini or the 4th house
- Malefic influence on the **4th house** or its lord
- **Mercury afflicted** by Saturn, Mars, Rahu, or Ketu
- **Weak, debilitated, or afflicted Moon**, often linked with anxiety-induced breathing issues
- Heavily afflicted **Ascendant** along with the **6th house** (disease house)

Such combinations may indicate asthma, bronchitis, chronic cough, breathing difficulty, or long-term lung weakness.

Astrological Remedies

(Spiritual support only – not a substitute for medical treatment)

Mantra Chanting

- **Mahamrityunjaya Mantra** – for healing, longevity, and protection:

Om Tryambakam Yajamahe Sugandhim Pushtivardhanam Urvarukamiva Bandhanan Mrityor Mukshiya Maamritat

- Chant **108 times daily** with faith and discipline.

Gem Therapy

(Only after proper horoscope analysis)

- **Emerald (Panna)** – if Mercury is weak or afflicted
- **Pearl (Moti)** – if Moon is weak
  Wear in silver on the little finger as advised by an astrologer.

Charity & Spiritual Practices

- Donate to the needy on **Wednesdays** (Mercury's day).
- Offer **milk, rice, or white sweets** to cows.
- Perform **Rudrabhishek** at a Shiva temple for health and vitality blessings.

Lifestyle & Yogic Support

- Practice **Pranayama** (Anulom-Vilom, Bhramari) under expert guidance.
- Maintain **clean, smoke-free surroundings**, as pollution directly affects lung energy.
- Reduce anxiety and stress, which strongly influence breathing patterns.

Chapter Insight

Lung-related disorders in astrology are primarily connected to **Mercury, Moon, the 4th house, and Gemini sign**, with chronic influence from **Saturn and Rahu**. Emotional stress, pollution, and long-standing planetary afflictions often act as triggers. While **medical diagnosis and treatment remain essential**, astrological remedies, pranayama, and disciplined lifestyle practices can offer **supportive healing and respiratory balance**.

Chapter 6

Digestive & Liver Disorders

11. Abdominal Pain (Udar Shoola) – An Integrated Ayurvedic, Astrological & Yogic Perspective

Introduction

Abdominal pain (**Udar Shoola**) is a very common yet clinically significant complaint that can arise from mild digestive disturbance to serious internal pathology. It may be acute or chronic, localized or generalized, and is often influenced by **dietary habits, stress, digestive fire, and emotional state**.

According to **Ayurveda**, abdominal pain is primarily associated with imbalance of **Vata, Pitta, and Kapha doshas**, with Vata playing a dominant role due to its connection with movement, gas, and pain. **Vedic Medical Astrology** further explains abdominal disorders through planetary influences governing digestion, intestines, metabolism, and emotional stress.

An integrated understanding allows early identification of disease tendency, recurrence, and recovery potential.

Common Causes of Abdominal Pain

(Medical Perspective)**

From a modern medical viewpoint, abdominal pain may occur due to:

- Digestive disorders such as gas, acidity, constipation, or indigestion
- Bacterial or viral infections
- Poor dietary habits (fried, spicy, or junk food)

- Psychological stress leading to cramps or burning sensation
- Excessive intake of spicy or acidic foods
- In some cases, it may indicate appendicitis, gastric ulcer, intestinal infection, or other internal disorders

Medical investigation becomes essential when pain is severe, persistent, or associated with fever, vomiting, or bleeding.

Ayurvedic Understanding of Abdominal Pain (Udar Shoola)

Ayurveda attributes abdominal pain to **disturbed Agni (digestive fire)** and accumulation of **Ama (toxins)**.

Dosha-wise Pain Patterns

- **Vata-type pain**: Cramping, gas, shifting pain
- **Pitta-type pain**: Burning sensation, acidity, inflammation
- **Kapha-type pain**: Heaviness, dull pain, sluggish digestion

Improper food combinations, irregular eating habits, stress, and seasonal imbalance aggravate doshas and weaken digestion.

Astrological Causes of Abdominal Pain

In **Medical Astrology**, abdominal pain is mainly associated with **Mars, Rahu, Ketu, Saturn, and the Moon**. These planets influence digestion, intestines, inflammation, obstruction, and emotional sensitivity.

Planetary Influences

Mars (Mangal)

- Represents heat, inflammation, and muscular activity
- When weak or afflicted in the **4th, 8th, or 12th house**, it may cause:
    - Abdominal inflammation
    - Acidity, burning sensation
    - Stress-related digestive disorders

Rahu

- Causes toxicity, infection, and irregular digestion
- Placement in the **8th or 12th house** may lead to:
    - Sudden abdominal pain
    - Infection or food-related intolerance
    - Pain with unclear or recurring cause

Ketu

- Indicates hidden or unexplained disorders
- When placed in the **8th house**, it may cause:
    - Abdominal cramps
    - Digestive instability
    - Pain without clear diagnosis

Saturn (Shani)

- Governs obstruction, dryness, and chronic conditions
- Placement in the **2nd or 6th house** may cause:
    - Constipation
    - Gas accumulation
    - Chronic digestive weakness

Moon (Chandra)

- Governs emotions, fluids, and gut-mind connection
- A weak Moon may result in:
    - Stress-induced abdominal pain
    - Anxiety-related indigestion
    - Irritable bowel tendencies

Abdominal pain often intensifies during adverse **Mahadasha, Antardasha, or planetary transits** involving these planets.

Yogic Support for Digestive Health

Yoga supports abdominal health by **stimulating digestion, reducing stress, and balancing Vata and Pitta**.

Recommended Yogic Practices

Asanas

- Pawanmuktasana – relieves gas and bloating
- Vajrasana – improves digestion after meals
- Bhujangasana – stimulates abdominal organs

Pranayama

- Anulom Vilom – calms nervous system
- Kapalbhati (mild, under guidance) – improves digestion

Meditation

- Reduces stress-related gut disorders
- Balances Moon and Vata energy

(Avoid intense yoga during acute pain or infection.)

Astrological Remedies for Abdominal Pain

Mars Affliction Remedies

- Offer **sesame seeds, jaggery, and chickpeas** to Lord Hanuman on Tuesdays
- Chant **"Om Kraam Kreem Kraum Sah Bhaumaya Namah"**
- Wear or carry a **red cloth**

Rahu Remedies

- Immerse a coconut in flowing water
- Donate **black sesame seeds**
- Chant **"Om Rahave Namah"**

Ketu Remedies

- Donate black sesame seeds on Saturdays

- Feed bread to black dogs
- Chant **"Om Kem Ketave Namah"**

Saturn Remedies

- Light a **mustard oil lamp under a Peepal tree** on Saturdays
- Chant **"Om Sham Shanaishcharaya Namah"**
- Donate black sesame seeds

These remedies help reduce planetary stress on digestion and intestines.

Ayurvedic & Home Remedies for Abdominal Pain

1. **Cumin and Dry Ginger Water**
    - Boil cumin seeds and dry ginger in water
    - Relieves gas and abdominal discomfort
2. **Mint Tea**
    - Boil mint leaves and consume warm
    - Improves digestion and reduces cramps
3. **Ginger Juice with Honey**
    - Reduces inflammation and abdominal pain
4. **Fennel and Mint**
    - Soothes digestive tract and reduces bloating
5. **Turmeric Milk**
    - Reduces inflammation and supports gut health
6. **Warm Water Bottle**
    - Relaxes abdominal muscles and relieves cramps

Preventive Guidelines

- Eat light, fresh, and easily digestible food

- Avoid overeating and incompatible food combinations
- Maintain regular meal timing
- Manage stress through yoga and meditation
- Strengthen digestive fire (Agni)

Ethical & Medical Disclaimer

Astrological, Ayurvedic, and Yogic remedies are **supportive and preventive** in nature. Persistent or severe abdominal pain must always be evaluated by a qualified medical professional.

Chapter Insight

Abdominal pain reflects a **complex interaction of digestion, planetary influence, emotional state, and lifestyle habits**. An integrated approach using **Medical Astrology, Ayurveda, and Yoga** allows accurate identification of root causes, prevention of recurrence, and holistic healing.

12. Gas and Acidity (Amlapitta & Vata Disorders) – An Integrated Ayurvedic, Astrological & Yogic Perspective

Introduction

Gas and acidity are among the most common digestive complaints in modern life. Though often ignored as minor discomforts, persistent gas, bloating, and acidity indicate **deep imbalance in digestion, metabolism, and mental state**. These conditions significantly affect quality of life and, if left untreated, may progress into chronic gastrointestinal disorders.

In **Ayurveda**, gas and acidity are primarily linked to **Pitta dosha imbalance**, often supported by aggravated **Vata**. **Vedic Medical Astrology** further explains these conditions through planetary afflictions that disturb digestion, emotional stability, and metabolic fire (**Agni**).

A holistic approach integrating **Ayurveda, Astrology, and Yoga** helps identify the root cause, recurrence pattern, and long-term prevention.

Common Causes of Gas and Acidity

(Medical Perspective)**

From a modern medical viewpoint, gas and acidity may arise due to:

- Poor dietary habits (excessively spicy, fried, sour, or junk food)
- Psychological stress and mental pressure
- Irregular daily routine and lack of proper sleep
- Excessive intake of acidic foods (tomatoes, citrus fruits, pickles)
- Overconsumption of tea, coffee, and carbonated drinks
- Digestive disorders such as acid reflux, gastritis, or gastric ulcer
- Side effects of certain medications affecting the stomach lining

While medications provide temporary relief, recurrence remains common unless the underlying cause is addressed.

Ayurvedic Understanding of Gas and Acidity

Ayurveda describes acidity as **Amlapitta**, caused by weakened or disturbed digestive fire (**Agni**) and accumulation of toxins (**Ama**).

Dosha-wise Contribution

- **Pitta aggravation** → burning sensation, acidity, sour belching
- **Vata aggravation** → gas, bloating, abdominal discomfort
- **Kapha involvement** → heaviness, sluggish digestion

Irregular eating habits, incompatible food combinations, emotional stress, and seasonal imbalance weaken digestion and promote acidity.

Astrological Causes of Gas and Acidity

In **Medical Astrology**, gas and acidity are primarily influenced by **Mars, Saturn, Rahu, Ketu, and the Moon**. These planets affect metabolism, intestines, inflammation, and emotional digestion.

Planetary Influences

Mars (Mangal)

- Represents fire, heat, and inflammation
- When afflicted in the **4th, 8th, or 12th house**, it may cause:
    - Excess acidity
    - Burning sensation
    - Stress-induced digestive imbalance

Saturn (Shani)

- Governs obstruction, dryness, and slow digestion
- Placement in the **2nd or 6th house** may result in:
    - Chronic gas
    - Constipation
    - Weak digestive capacity

Rahu and Ketu

- Represent toxicity, confusion, and hidden imbalance
- When placed in the **8th or 12th house**, they may cause:

    - Irregular digestion
    - Gas and acidity without clear dietary reason
    - Recurrent digestive disturbances

Moon (Chandra)

- Governs emotional digestion and gut-mind axis
- A weak Moon may lead to:
    - Stress-related acidity
    - Anxiety-induced gas
    - Emotional eating disorders

Digestive symptoms often worsen during adverse **Mahadasha, Antardasha, or planetary transits** involving these planets.

Yogic Support for Digestive Balance

Yoga helps by **strengthening digestive fire, calming the nervous system, and balancing Pitta and Vata**.

Recommended Yogic Practices

Asanas

- Vajrasana – improves digestion after meals
- Pawanmuktasana – relieves gas and bloating
- Ardha Matsyendrasana – stimulates digestive organs

Pranayama

- Anulom Vilom – balances nervous and digestive systems
- Sheetali / Sheetkari – cools excess Pitta
- Bhramari – reduces stress-induced acidity

Meditation

- Reduces emotional stress affecting digestion
- Strengthens Moon energy

(Avoid intense practices during severe acidity.)

Astrological Remedies for Gas and Acidity

Mars Affliction Remedies

- Offer **sesame seeds, jaggery, and chickpeas** to Lord Hanuman on Tuesdays
- Chant **"Om Kraam Kreem Kraum Sah Bhaumaya Namah"**
- Wear or carry a **red cloth**

Saturn Remedies

- Light a **mustard oil lamp under a Peepal tree** on Saturdays
- Donate **black sesame seeds**
- Chant **"Om Sham Shanaishcharaya Namah"**

Rahu Remedies

- Immerse a coconut in flowing water
- Donate black sesame seeds
- Chant **"Om Rahave Namah"**

Ketu Remedies

- Donate black sesame seeds on Saturdays
- Feed bread to black dogs
- Chant **"Om Kem Ketave Namah"**

These remedies help pacify planetary stress affecting digestion and metabolism.

Ayurvedic & Home Remedies for Gas and Acidity

1. **Cumin and Dry Ginger Water**
    - Boil cumin seeds and dry ginger in water
    - Relieves gas and acidity
2. **Mint Tea**
    - Provides cooling effect and improves digestion

3. **Ginger Juice with Honey**
    - Reduces inflammation and supports digestion
4. **Fennel and Mint**
    - Soothes digestive tract and reduces bloating
5. **Lemon Water with Salt**
    - Balances acidity when taken moderately
6. **Turmeric Milk**
    - Reduces inflammation and strengthens digestion
7. **Adequate Hydration**
    - Maintains digestive balance and reduces acidity

Preventive Guidelines

- Eat fresh, light, and easily digestible food
- Avoid overeating and late-night meals
- Reduce caffeine and carbonated drinks
- Maintain disciplined daily routine
- Manage stress through yoga and meditation

Ethical & Medical Disclaimer

Astrological, Ayurvedic, and Yogic remedies are **supportive and preventive tools**. Chronic or severe acidity must always be evaluated and treated by a qualified medical professional.

Chapter Insight

Gas and acidity are not merely digestive complaints but **signals of disturbed Agni, emotional stress, and planetary imbalance**. An integrated approach using **Medical Astrology, Ayurveda, and Yoga** provides sustainable relief, prevention, and digestive harmony.

13. Indigestion (Ajirna) – An Integrated Ayurvedic, Astrological & Yogic Perspective

Introduction

Indigestion (**Ajirna**) is a common digestive disorder in which food is not properly digested, leading to symptoms such as heaviness, bloating, gas, burning sensation, and discomfort in the abdomen. Though often ignored, persistent indigestion indicates a **weakened digestive fire (Agni)** and deeper imbalance within the body.

According to **Ayurveda**, indigestion arises due to imbalance of **Vata, Pitta, and Kapha doshas**, while **Vedic Medical Astrology** attributes recurrent or chronic indigestion to specific **planetary afflictions** that disturb digestion, metabolism, and mental stability. An integrated understanding helps identify not only the cause, but also **why digestion weakens repeatedly in certain individuals**.

Common Causes of Indigestion

(Medical Perspective)**

From a modern medical viewpoint, indigestion may occur due to:

- Poor dietary habits (excessively spicy, fried, oily, or heavy food)
- Lying down immediately after meals or drinking excessive water post-meal
- Psychological stress and mental pressure affecting gut function
- Weak intestines or impaired digestive capacity
- Conditions such as gastric ulcer or acid reflux
- Lack of dietary fiber or irregular eating habits

If indigestion becomes frequent, it may indicate an underlying gastrointestinal disorder requiring medical evaluation.

Ayurvedic Understanding of Indigestion (Ajirna)

Ayurveda considers indigestion as a direct consequence of **disturbed Agni** and accumulation of **Ama (toxins)**.

Dosha-wise Indigestion Patterns

- **Vata-type Ajirna**: Gas, bloating, irregular digestion
- **Pitta-type Ajirna**: Burning sensation, sour belching, acidity
- **Kapha-type Ajirna**: Heaviness, sluggish digestion, lethargy

Irregular food timing, incompatible food combinations, stress, and seasonal imbalance weaken digestion and lead to chronic indigestion.

Astrological Causes of Indigestion

In **Medical Astrology**, indigestion is mainly associated with **Mars, Saturn, Rahu, Ketu, and the Moon**. These planets influence digestion, metabolism, intestinal function, and emotional digestion.

Planetary Influences

Mars (Mangal)

- Represents digestive fire, heat, and inflammation
- When weak or afflicted in the **4th, 8th, or 12th house**, it may cause:
    - Disturbed digestion
    - Inflammatory gastric conditions
    - Stress-related indigestion

Saturn (Shani)

- Governs delay, obstruction, and chronic weakness
- Placement in the **2nd or 6th house** may lead to:
    - Slow digestion
    - Gas, constipation, and chronic indigestion

Rahu and Ketu

- Represent irregularity, toxicity, and hidden imbalance
- When placed in the **8th or 12th house**, they may cause:
    - Sudden or unexplained indigestion
    - Digestive disturbance without clear dietary cause

Moon (Chandra)

- Governs emotions, fluids, and gut-mind connection
- A weak Moon may result in:
    - Stress-induced indigestion
    - Emotional eating
    - Loss of digestive rhythm

Indigestion often worsens during adverse **Mahadasha, Antardasha, or planetary transits** of these planets.

Yogic Support for Digestive Strength

Yoga plays a vital role in improving digestion by **stimulating abdominal organs, calming the nervous system, and strengthening Agni**.

Recommended Yogic Practices

Asanas

- Vajrasana – improves digestion after meals
- Pawanmuktasana – relieves gas and bloating
- Malasana – supports intestinal movement

Pranayama

- Anulom Vilom – balances digestion and stress
- Bhramari – reduces anxiety affecting digestion
- Mild Kapalbhati (under guidance) – stimulates Agni

Meditation

- Stabilizes Moon energy
- Reduces stress-related digestive disturbance

Astrological Remedies for Indigestion

Mars Affliction Remedies

- Offer **sesame seeds, jaggery, and chickpeas** to Lord Hanuman on Tuesdays
- Chant **"Om Kraam Kreem Kraum Sah Bhaumaya Namah"**
- Wear or carry a **red cloth**

Saturn Remedies

- Light a **mustard oil lamp under a Peepal tree** on Saturdays
- Donate **black sesame seeds**
- Chant **"Om Sham Shanaishcharaya Namah"**

Rahu Remedies

- Immerse a coconut in flowing water
- Donate black sesame seeds
- Chant **"Om Rahave Namah"**

Ketu Remedies

- Donate black sesame seeds on Saturdays
- Feed bread to black dogs
- Chant **"Om Kem Ketave Namah"**

Moon Strengthening Remedies

- Donate milk and rice on Mondays
- Chant **"Om Sham Chandramase Namah"**

These remedies help stabilize digestion by balancing planetary energies.

Ayurvedic & Home Remedies for Indigestion

1. **Ginger Therapy**
    - Fresh ginger or ginger tea strengthens digestion
2. **Cumin and Dry Ginger Water**
    - Improves digestion and relieves indigestion
3. **Mint Tea**
    - Calms stomach and reduces gas

4. **Fennel and Cumin Water**
    - Enhances digestion and reduces heaviness
5. **Tulsi Leaves**
    - Improve digestion and reduce stress-related indigestion
6. **Turmeric Milk**
    - Strengthens digestive system and reduces inflammation
7. **Amla with Honey**
    - Improves digestion and balances Pitta
8. **Light Walking After Meals**
    - Enhances digestive process
9. **Adequate Hydration**
    - Maintains digestive balance (avoid excess water immediately after meals)

Preventive Guidelines

- Eat fresh, warm, and easily digestible food
- Maintain regular meal timings
- Avoid incompatible food combinations
- Manage stress through yoga and meditation
- Respect digestive capacity (Agni)

Ethical & Medical Disclaimer

Astrological, Ayurvedic, and Yogic remedies are **supportive and preventive** in nature. Recurrent or severe indigestion should always be evaluated by a qualified medical professional.

Chapter Insight

Indigestion is not merely a digestive complaint but a **reflection of weakened Agni, emotional imbalance, and planetary influence**. An integrated approach using **Medical Astrology, Ayurveda, and Yoga** allows lasting digestive health, prevention of recurrence, and holistic well-being.

14. Diarrhea (Atisara) – An Integrated Ayurvedic, Astrological & Yogic Perspective

Introduction

Diarrhea (**Atisara**) is a common digestive disorder characterized by frequent passage of loose or watery stools. It leads to weakness, dehydration, electrolyte imbalance, and reduced digestive strength if not managed properly. While acute diarrhea may resolve quickly, recurrent or prolonged diarrhea indicates **deep imbalance in digestion, immunity, and internal energy systems**.

According to **Ayurveda**, diarrhea is caused by imbalance of **Vata, Pitta, and Kapha doshas**, particularly involving disturbed digestive fire (**Agni**) and intestinal weakness. **Vedic Medical Astrology** further explains diarrhea through **planetary afflictions** that disturb digestion, intestinal absorption, immunity, and mental stability.

An integrated approach helps understand **why diarrhea occurs repeatedly in certain individuals**, even with similar dietary exposure.

Common Causes of Diarrhea

(Medical Perspective)**

From a modern medical viewpoint, diarrhea may occur due to:

- Viral or bacterial infections (such as viral gastroenteritis, typhoid, amoebiasis)
- Consumption of contaminated or spoiled food
- Psychological stress affecting intestinal motility
- Inflammation or ulceration of intestines (Crohn's disease, IBS)
- Food poisoning due to contaminated food or water
- Excessive intake of spicy, sour, or irritant foods
- Side effects of antibiotics or other medications

Persistent diarrhea requires medical evaluation to prevent dehydration and nutritional deficiency.

Ayurvedic Understanding of Diarrhea (Atisara)

Ayurveda defines diarrhea as **Atisara**, caused by:

- Weak or disturbed **Agni (digestive fire)**
- Accumulation of **Ama (toxins)**
- Excess movement of **Vata** in the intestines

Dosha-wise Diarrhea Patterns

- **Vata-type Atisara**: Frequent stools, gas, abdominal cramps
- **Pitta-type Atisara**: Burning sensation, yellowish stools, dehydration
- **Kapha-type Atisara**: Thick stools, mucus, heaviness

Improper diet, emotional stress, fear, and seasonal imbalance weaken digestion and disturb intestinal absorption.

Astrological Causes of Diarrhea

In **Medical Astrology**, diarrhea is mainly associated with **Rahu, Ketu, Mars, Saturn, and the Moon**. These planets influence intestines, immunity, fluids, and metabolic balance.

Planetary Influences

Rahu

- Represents toxicity, infection, and irregular functioning
- When placed in the **8th or 12th house**, it may cause:
  - Intestinal infection
  - Sudden or unexplained diarrhea
  - Stress-induced digestive imbalance

Ketu

- Causes hidden weakness and unpredictable disorders
- Placement in the **8th or 12th house** may lead to:
  - Chronic or recurrent diarrhea

- Poor absorption of nutrients
- Intestinal sensitivity

Mars (Mangal)

- Governs heat, inflammation, and muscular activity
- When afflicted in the **4th, 8th, or 12th house**, it may result in:
  - Inflammatory diarrhea
  - Burning sensation
  - Diarrhea triggered by anger or stress

Saturn (Shani)

- Governs obstruction and chronic imbalance
- Placement in the **2nd or 6th house** may cause:
  - Weak digestion
  - Alternating constipation and diarrhea
  - Long-term intestinal weakness

Moon (Chandra) ***(implicit influence)***

- Governs fluids, emotions, and gut-mind axis
- A weak Moon may cause:
  - Stress-related diarrhea
  - Emotional instability affecting digestion

Diarrhea often worsens during adverse **Mahadasha, Antardasha, or planetary transits** involving these planets.

Yogic Support for Intestinal Stability

Yoga supports recovery by **calming intestinal movement, strengthening digestion, and reducing stress**.

Recommended Yogic Practices

Asanas

- Vajrasana – stabilizes digestion
- Pawanmuktasana – relieves gas and cramps
- Shavasana – relaxes nervous system

Pranayama

- Anulom Vilom – balances digestion and stress
- Bhramari – calms gut-brain connection

Meditation

- Reduces anxiety-induced intestinal disturbance

(Avoid intense yoga during acute diarrhea.)

6. Astrological Remedies for Diarrhea

Rahu Remedies

- Immerse a coconut in flowing water
- Donate black sesame seeds
- Chant **"Om Rahave Namah"**

Ketu Remedies

- Donate black sesame seeds on Saturdays
- Feed bread to black dogs
- Light a white lamp at home
- Chant **"Om Kem Ketave Namah"**

Mars Remedies

- Offer sesame seeds, jaggery, and chickpeas to Lord Hanuman on Tuesdays
- Chant **"Om Kraam Kreem Kraum Sah Bhaumaya Namah"**
- Wear or carry a red cloth

Saturn Remedies

- Light a mustard oil lamp under a Peepal tree on Saturdays

- Donate black sesame seeds and black clothes
- Chant **"Om Sham Shanaishcharaya Namah"**

These remedies help stabilize intestinal function by pacifying planetary imbalance.

Ayurvedic & Home Remedies for Diarrhea

1. **Banana and Curd**
    - Strengthens intestines and restores gut bacteria
2. **Amla**
    - Regulates digestion and reduces diarrhea
3. **Turmeric Water**
    - Reduces intestinal infection due to antibacterial properties
4. **Fennel Water**
    - Calms intestines and reduces stool frequency
5. **Tamarind Water**
    - Improves digestion when taken mildly
6. **Rice Water**
    - Controls diarrhea and restores energy
7. **Ginger and Honey**
    - Improves digestion and reduces cramps
8. **Adequate Hydration**
    - Prevents dehydration and electrolyte imbalance
9. **Coconut Water**
    - Replenishes fluids and minerals naturally

Preventive Guidelines

- Maintain strict personal hygiene
- Drink clean, boiled, or filtered water
- Avoid stale or outside food
- Consume light, freshly prepared meals
- Manage stress and emotional instability

Ethical & Medical Disclaimer

Astrological, Ayurvedic, and Yogic remedies are **supportive and preventive**. Diarrhea caused by infection, dehydration, or prolonged symptoms must always be treated under professional medical supervision.

Chapter Insight

Diarrhea reflects a **disturbance of digestion, intestinal absorption, emotional balance, and planetary influence**. An integrated approach using **Medical Astrology, Ayurveda, and Yoga** provides deeper understanding, prevention, and sustainable recovery

15. Constipation (Malabandha) – Astrological, Ayurvedic & Holistic Remedies

Introduction

Constipation (**Malabandha**) is one of the most common yet neglected digestive disorders. It is characterized by **infrequent bowel movements, hard stools, straining, and a feeling of incomplete evacuation**. While diet and lifestyle play an important role, chronic constipation often has **psychological, neurological, and astrological roots**.

In **Ayurveda**, constipation is primarily linked to **Vata imbalance**, while **Vedic Medical Astrology** explains it through **planetary influences affecting digestion, water balance, intestinal movement, and nervous control**.

Understanding constipation through an integrated lens helps identify **why some individuals suffer chronically despite good diet**.

Constipation – Medical Overview

From a modern medical perspective, constipation may be caused by:

- Low fiber intake
- Insufficient water consumption
- Sedentary lifestyle
- Stress, anxiety, or depression
- Suppression of natural urges
- Side effects of medications
- Weak intestinal peristalsis

Chronic constipation can lead to **piles, fissures, acidity, headaches, and toxin accumulation**.

Ayurvedic Understanding of Constipation

In Ayurveda, constipation occurs due to:

- **Vata Dosha aggravation** (dryness, roughness, obstruction)

- Weak digestive fire (**Mandagni**)
- Accumulation of **Ama (toxins)**

Dosha Involvement

- **Vata-type constipation**: Dry, hard stools, gas, bloating
- **Pitta-type constipation**: Burning sensation, acidity, irritation
- **Kapha-type constipation**: Sluggish digestion, heaviness

Mental stress, fear, irregular routine, and dehydration worsen the condition.

Astrological Causes of Constipation

Constipation is strongly associated with **Saturn, Rahu, Ketu, Moon**, and afflicted digestive houses.

Key Astrological Factors

6th House (Disease House)

- Represents digestion, intestines, and daily health
- Malefic planets here cause chronic bowel disorders

Saturn (Shani)

- Planet of slowness, dryness, obstruction
- When influencing **2nd, 5th, or 6th house**, it may cause:
    - Hard stools
    - Delayed bowel movements
    - Chronic constipation

Rahu & Ketu

- Cause irregular digestion and toxin buildup
- Can lead to:
    - Gas, bloating, constipation
    - Nervous-related bowel dysfunction

Moon (Chandra)

- Governs body fluids and gut-mind connection
- Weak Moon leads to:
    - Dehydration
    - Stress-induced constipation

Lagnesh & 5th House Weakness

- Reduces digestive strength (**Agni**)
- Causes poor absorption and intestinal inactivity

Constipation often worsens during **Saturn or Rahu-Ketu Mahadasha/Antardasha**.

Yogic Role in Constipation Management

Yoga helps by **stimulating intestinal movement, improving nerve control, and reducing mental stress**.

Recommended Practices

Asanas

- Pawanmuktasana – activates intestines
- Malasana – improves bowel movement
- Vajrasana – strengthens digestion

Pranayama

- Anulom Vilom – balances nervous system
- Bhastrika (mild) – stimulates digestive fire

Meditation

- Reduces stress-related bowel suppression

Astrological Remedies for Constipation

Saturn Remedies

- Donate black lentils on Saturdays

- Light mustard oil lamp under Peepal tree
- Chant **"Om Sham Shanaishcharaya Namah"** (108 times)

Moon Strengthening Remedies

- Donate white items (milk, rice, sugar) on Mondays
- Offer water to the Moon at night
- Chant **"Om Cham Chandraya Namah"**

Sun Remedies (Digestive Fire)

- Offer water to the Sun every morning with red flower
- Chant **"Om Ghrini Suryaya Namah"**

Rahu-Ketu Remedies

- Donate coconut for Rahu
- Feed bread to dogs for Ketu
- Chant:
    - **"Om Raam Rahave Namah"**
    - **"Om Kem Ketave Namah"**

These remedies help restore **intestinal rhythm and digestive vitality**.

Ayurvedic & Home Remedies

1. **Warm Water Intake**
    - Drink lukewarm water, especially on waking
2. **Triphala Churna**
    - 1 teaspoon at night with warm water
3. **Soaked Raisins**
    - 4–5 soaked raisins every morning
4. **Abdominal Oil Massage**
    - Gentle navel-area massage with warm oil

5. **Fiber-Rich Diet**
    - Fruits, vegetables, whole grains
6. **Regular Bowel Routine**
    - Fixed timing helps regulate intestines

Preventive Lifestyle Guidelines

- Maintain hydration throughout the day
- Avoid suppressing natural urges
- Eat at regular times
- Reduce mental stress
- Maintain daily physical movement

Ethical & Medical Disclaimer

Astrological and Ayurvedic remedies are **supportive measures**. Chronic or severe constipation, bleeding, or sudden changes in bowel habits require **medical evaluation**.

Chapter Insight

Constipation is not merely a digestive disorder—it reflects **Vata imbalance, emotional stress, water deficiency, and planetary obstruction**. Healing is most effective when **Astrology, Ayurveda, Yoga, and Lifestyle correction work together**.

16. Mouth Ulcers (Aphthous Ulcers / Oral Ulcers) – An Integrated Astrological, Ayurvedic & Yogic Perspective

Introduction

Mouth ulcers are **small, painful sores** that develop inside the mouth—on the tongue, inner cheeks, gums, lips, or palate. Though usually not serious, recurrent or severe ulcers can indicate **systemic, nutritional, or astrological imbalances**.

Medical Perspective

Symptoms:

- Painful white or yellow sores with red borders
- Burning or stinging sensation while eating or speaking
- Swelling or tenderness in the mouth
- Difficulty chewing spicy, salty, or acidic foods
- Recurrent ulcers (chronic tendency)
- Occasionally fever or fatigue (in severe cases)

Primary Causes:

- **Vitamin deficiencies** (B12, Iron, Folic Acid)
- Excess **heat (Pitta imbalance)** in the body
- Stress, anxiety, or emotional suppression
- Hormonal changes
- Weak immunity
- Mouth injury, sharp teeth, or dental braces
- Certain medications
- Digestive disorders and acidity
- Autoimmune conditions (in rare cases)

Astrological Perspective

Mouth ulcers are closely related to **fire, speech organs, digestion, and blood quality**.

Key Planets & Their Roles:

- Sun – Heat, ulcers, inflammation
- Mars – Pitta, wounds, sores
- Mercury – Mouth, speech, oral cavity
- Venus – Body fluids, healing capacity
- Rahu – Toxicity, infections, chronic recurrence of disease.

Key Houses & Their Significance:

- 2nd House – Mouth, speech, oral health
- 6th House – Disease, ulcers, infections, enemies within the body (pathology)
- 1st House – Overall immunity, vitality, and constitutional strength.

Astrological Combinations Indicating Susceptibility:

- Affliction of **2nd house** by Sun, Mars, or Rahu
- **Sun–Mars conjunction** affecting 2nd or 6th house
- Weak or afflicted **Mercury** (speech & mouth)
- Rahu influence causing **recurrent or non-healing ulcers**
- Excessive fire signs (Aries, Leo, Sagittarius) dominance
- Weak Venus leading to delayed healing

Astrological Remedies

Sun & Mars Pacification:

- Offer water to the Sun daily using a copper vessel
- Mantra:
  "Om Ghrini Suryaya Namah" – 108 times
- Avoid anger, excessive heat, and spicy foods

☿ Mercury Strengthening:

- Chant:
  "Om Budhaya Namah" – 108 times
- Donate green moong or green vegetables on Wednesday

☊ Rahu Shanti:

- Chant:
  "Om Raam Rahave Namah"
- Donate black sesame seeds or mustard oil
- Avoid intoxicants and junk food

Gemstone Remedies

(Only after proper horoscope analysis)

- **Emerald** – For Mercury-related mouth disorders
- **Pearl** – To cool excessive heat and balance Moon
- **Diamond / Opal** – If Venus is weak (healing issues)

Avoid Ruby or Red Coral without expert consultation, as they may increase heat.

Yogic & Ayurvedic Support

Yogic Practices:

- **Sheetali & Sheetkari Pranayama** – Reduces body heat
- **Chandra Bhedana** – Cooling pranayama
- Meditation for stress control

Ayurvedic Measures:

- Triphala water mouth rinse
- Honey + turmeric application on ulcers
- Licorice (Mulethi) powder with honey

- Coconut oil pulling (Gandusha)
- Avoid late nights and overheating foods

Dietary Recommendations:

- Cooling foods: cucumber, coconut water, buttermilk
- Vitamin B-rich foods: banana, whole grains, sprouts
- Iron-rich foods: dates, raisins, spinach
- Plenty of water
- Avoid:
    - Spicy, fried, acidic foods
    - Excess tea, coffee, alcohol
    - Smoking and tobacco

Chapter Insight:

Mouth ulcers are **not merely local oral issues**; they reflect **internal heat, digestive imbalance, emotional stress, and planetary afflictions**—especially involving the **Sun, Mars, Mercury, and Rahu**. A combined approach of **medical care, diet correction, yogic cooling, and astrological balance** ensures lasting relief and prevents recurrence.

Chapter 7

Kidney & Urinary Disorders

(Reserved for future diseases)

Chapter 8

Bone, Joint & Musculoskeletal Disorders

(Reserved for future diseases)

Chapter 9

Skin & Allergy Disorders

17. Skin Allergy (Twak Rog) – Astrological Causes, Medical Understanding & Holistic Remedies

Introduction

Skin allergies are among the most visible expressions of internal imbalance in the human body. They may appear as **itching, rashes, redness, swelling, hives, eczema, or recurring infections**. While modern medicine attributes skin allergies to immune reactions, chemicals, food sensitivity, or environmental exposure, **Medical Astrology recognizes skin disorders as a reflection of planetary disturbances, emotional stress, and toxin accumulation.**

In Ayurveda, skin diseases are collectively known as **Twak Rog**, primarily linked to **Pitta and Rakta (blood) imbalance**, with secondary involvement of **Vata and Kapha**. Astrologically, skin represents the **protective boundary of the body**, governed by specific planets and houses.

Medical Perspective on Skin Allergies

From a clinical standpoint, skin allergies may arise due to:

- Food intolerance or drug reactions
- Environmental allergens (dust, pollen, chemicals)
- Autoimmune responses
- Hormonal imbalance
- Stress-induced immune dysfunction

Common manifestations include:

- Contact dermatitis

- Urticaria (hives)
- Atopic eczema
- Allergic rashes
- Chronic itching

Persistent skin allergies indicate **systemic imbalance rather than a local skin issue**.

Ayurvedic Understanding of Skin Allergies

Ayurveda considers skin diseases as a result of:

- **Aggravated Pitta Dosha** – heat, inflammation, redness
- **Impure Rakta Dhatu (blood toxins)**
- **Ama (undigested toxins)** circulating in the body

Dosha-wise Skin Allergy Patterns

- **Pitta-dominant**: Burning, redness, inflammation, itching
- **Kapha-dominant**: Oozing, swelling, heaviness
- **Vata-dominant**: Dryness, cracking, scaling

Mental stress, anger, fear, and suppressed emotions significantly worsen skin conditions.

Astrological Causes of Skin Allergies

Skin allergies are strongly connected with **shadow planets, chronic malefics, and emotional instability**.

Key Astrological Factors

Rahu and Ketu

- Primary planets responsible for:
    - Allergies
    - Sudden eruptions
    - Autoimmune and toxic reactions

- Rahu especially causes **unpredictable, recurring skin allergies** and hypersensitivity.

Saturn (Shani)

- Causes **chronic, long-standing, non-healing skin disorders**
- Associated with dryness, pigmentation, scaling, and thickened skin
- Saturn's influence makes conditions persistent and resistant to treatment.

Moon (Chandra) and Emotional Health

- Moon governs:
    - Body fluids
    - Immunity
    - Mind–skin connection
- A weak or afflicted Moon causes:
    - Stress-triggered allergies
    - Emotional suppression manifesting on skin

Sixth House (Rog Bhava)

- House of disease and immunity
- Presence or aspect of **Rahu, Ketu, Saturn, or Mars** here often results in:
    - Skin diseases
    - Allergic disorders
    - Inflammatory conditions

Mars (Secondary Factor)

- Excess heat, inflammation, and rashes
- Mars with Rahu often causes **aggressive allergic reactions**

Skin allergies often intensify during **Rahu–Ketu or Saturn Mahadasha/Antardasha**.

Astrological Remedies for Skin Allergies

Rahu Pacification Remedies

- Chant every Saturday:
  "Om Bhraam Bhreem Bhraum Sah Rahave Namah" – 108 times
- Flow a coconut in running water
- Avoid intoxication, junk food, and excessive chemicals

Saturn Remedies

- On Saturdays, donate mustard oil after seeing your reflection in it
- Light a lamp in Shani temple or under Peepal tree
- Practice patience and disciplined routine

Strengthening the Moon

- Donate milk and rice on Mondays
- Chant:
  "Om Som Somaya Namah"
- Maintain emotional balance and proper sleep

Lifestyle Precautions (Astrological)

- Avoid red clothes, red chilies, and aggressive colors if Mars–Rahu is afflicted
- Drink water stored in a copper vessel to balance Moon and skin health

Ayurvedic & Natural Remedies (Supportive Care)

These remedies support healing alongside astrological correction:

- **Aloe Vera Gel** – cools Pitta and reduces inflammation
- **Turmeric Paste** – antibacterial and blood-purifying
- **Neem Leaves Paste or Bath** – detoxifies blood and skin
- Wash skin with **clean, fresh water**

- Avoid excessive cosmetics and chemical products

Dietary discipline is crucial: avoid spicy, fermented, oily, and packaged foods.

Preventive & Lifestyle Guidelines

- Maintain gut health (skin and gut are directly linked)
- Manage stress through meditation and pranayama
- Follow regular sleep cycle
- Avoid suppressing emotions
- Maintain hygiene without over-cleansing

Medical & Ethical Disclaimer

Skin allergies may sometimes indicate **serious immune or systemic conditions**. Astrological and Ayurvedic remedies are **supportive and complementary**, not a replacement for medical diagnosis. Persistent, spreading, or infected skin conditions must be evaluated by a qualified dermatologist.

Chapter Insight

Skin allergies are **not merely external reactions**, but signals of **planetary imbalance, emotional overload, toxin accumulation, and immune sensitivity**. True healing occurs when **Astrology, Ayurveda, mental health, and lifestyle correction work together**.

Chapter 10

Neurological Disorders

18. Headache (Shiroroga) – An Integrated Ayurvedic, Astrological & Yogic Perspective

Introduction

Headache (**Shiroroga**) is one of the most common yet complex health complaints experienced by individuals of all ages. Though often perceived as a minor ailment, recurrent or chronic headaches indicate **deeper physical, mental, or energetic imbalance**. Headaches may arise due to lifestyle stress, hormonal changes, neurological strain, or environmental factors.

Ayurveda explains headaches as a disorder caused by **imbalance of Vata, Pitta, and Kapha doshas**, while **Vedic Medical Astrology** identifies specific planetary afflictions responsible for pain, pressure, and mental disturbance. Understanding both perspectives allows accurate identification of **cause, recurrence, and remedy**.

Common Causes of Headache

(Medical Perspective)**

From a medical standpoint, headaches may occur due to:

- Mental stress, anxiety, or emotional pressure
- Eye strain due to excessive screen time or prolonged focus
- Sleep deprivation or irregular sleep patterns
- Environmental changes, especially weather fluctuations
- Hormonal imbalance (commonly during menstruation in women)
- High or low blood pressure

- Migraine, tension headache, or sinus-related headache

Modern medicine treats symptoms effectively, but often does not address **individual susceptibility or repetitive occurrence**, which astrology and Ayurveda clarify.

Ayurvedic Understanding of Headache (Shiroroga)

Ayurveda classifies headaches according to **dosha dominance**:

- **Vata-type headache**: Sharp pain, dryness, restlessness
- **Pitta-type headache**: Burning sensation, throbbing pain, sensitivity to light
- **Kapha-type headache**: Heavy sensation, dull pain, congestion

Improper digestion, mental stress, suppressed emotions, and seasonal imbalance aggravate doshas, leading to headache manifestation.

Astrological Causes of Headache

In **Medical Astrology**, headache is strongly influenced by **Mars, Saturn, Rahu, Ketu, and the Moon**. These planets govern **head region, nervous system, blood flow, and mental stability**.

Planetary Influences

Mars (Mangal)

- Governs blood, heat, aggression, and head region
- When weak or afflicted in the **4th, 8th, or 12th house**, it may cause:
    - Severe headaches
    - Stress-induced pain
    - Migraine related to anger or suppressed emotions

Saturn (Shani)

- Represents pressure, tension, and chronic suffering
- Placement in the **2nd or 4th house** can lead to:
    - Persistent headaches

- Mental fatigue
- Stress-related neurological strain

Rahu

- Causes confusion, anxiety, and unnatural pressure
- When placed in the **8th or 12th house**, it may result in:
    - Sudden headaches
    - Restlessness and panic-related pain
    - Sleep-related headache disorders

Ketu

- Associated with detachment, fear, and internal confusion
- Can cause:
    - Unexplained headaches
    - Pain linked to mental disturbance or fear

Moon (Chandra)

- Governs mind, fluids, emotions, and nervous balance
- A weak Moon, especially in the **6th or 8th house**, may cause:
    - Emotional instability
    - Stress-triggered headaches
    - Hormonal or cyclical headaches

Headaches often intensify during **adverse Mahadasha, Antardasha, or planetary transits** involving these planets.

Yogic Support for Headache Relief

Yoga helps by **calming the nervous system, improving circulation, and reducing mental stress**.

Recommended Yogic Practices

Pranayama

- Anulom Vilom – balances nervous system
- Bhramari – highly effective for stress-related headaches
- Sheetali – useful in Pitta-dominant headaches

Asanas

- Shavasana
- Balasana (Child's Pose)
- Sukhasana with deep breathing

Meditation

- Reduces mental overload and emotional tension
- Stabilizes Moon-related disturbances

(Yoga should be practiced gently and regularly, avoiding strain.)

Astrological Remedies for Headache

Mars Affliction Remedies

- Offer **sesame seeds, jaggery, and chickpeas** to Lord Hanuman on Tuesdays
- Chant **"Om Kraam Kreem Kraum Sah Bhaumaya Namah"** (108 times)
- Wear or carry a **red cloth** to strengthen Mars energy

Saturn Affliction Remedies

- Light a **mustard oil lamp under a Peepal tree** on Saturdays
- Donate **black sesame seeds**
- Chant **"Om Sham Shanaishcharaya Namah"**

Rahu Remedies

- Immerse a coconut in flowing water
- Chant **"Om Rahave Namah"**

Ketu Remedies

- Donate black sesame seeds on Saturdays
- Feed bread to black dogs
- Chant **"Om Kem Ketave Namah"**

These remedies gradually reduce planetary pressure and mental strain.

Ayurvedic & Home Remedies for Headache

1. **Ginger Therapy**
    - Ginger tea improves circulation and pacifies Vata
    - Boil ginger in water and consume warm
2. **Adequate Hydration**
    - Dehydration is a major headache trigger
    - Drink sufficient water throughout the day
3. **Lemon Water**
    - Mix lemon juice with a pinch of salt in water
    - Provides quick relief in fatigue-related headaches
4. **Tulsi and Clove Decoction**
    - Boil tulsi leaves with cloves
    - Calms mind and relieves tension
5. **Clove Chewing**
    - Chewing 1–2 cloves helps reduce pain naturally
6. **Amla and Honey**
    - Amla powder with honey is effective for Pitta-type headaches

Preventive Guidelines

- Maintain proper sleep cycle

- Reduce excessive screen exposure
- Control stress through meditation
- Follow seasonal dietary discipline
- Strengthen Moon through mental balance

Ethical & Medical Disclaimer

Astrological, Ayurvedic, and Yogic remedies are **supportive and preventive tools**. They must always be used **alongside professional medical advice**, especially in cases of chronic or severe headache.

Chapter Insight

Headache is not merely a physical condition but a **reflection of planetary pressure, doshic imbalance, and mental stress**. An integrated approach using **Medical Astrology, Ayurveda, and Yoga** enables accurate identification of root cause, recurrence pattern, and sustainable relief.

19. Ocular Migraine – An Integrated Astrological, Ayurvedic & Yogic Perspective

Introduction

Ocular Migraine is a temporary eye disorder in which a person experiences blurred vision, flickering lights, blind spots, or zigzag patterns in vision. It may occur with or without headache. The condition usually resolves within 30 minutes on its own, but frequent occurrences require medical attention. An integrated approach combining Medical, Astrological, Ayurvedic, and Yogic insights helps in managing triggers, preventing recurrence, and supporting eye health.

Medical Perspective

Symptoms:

- Flickering lights or scintillations in vision
- Zigzag lines
- Temporary partial or full vision loss in one eye
- Headache (sometimes absent)
- Nausea, dizziness

Primary Causes:

- Constriction and dilation of brain and ocular blood vessels
- Stress and lack of sleep
- Hormonal changes (especially in women)
- Exposure to bright lights or excessive screen time

Treatment:

- Avoid triggers such as bright screens and lights
- Migraine medications (e.g., Triptans, Beta-blockers)
- Consultation with ophthalmologist and neurologist is recommended

Astrological Perspective

Key Planets & Houses:

- Moon (Chandra) – Governs mental state and nervous system
- Sun (Surya) – Represents vision, light, and head
- Ketu – Associated with confusion, illusion, and shadow effects
- Rahu – Main factor for migraine and mental confusion
- 4th House – Mental and emotional state
- 12th House – Eye disorders and head problems

Astrological Combinations Indicating Susceptibility:

- Malefic aspects or conjunctions of Shani/Rahu on Moon, Sun, Rahu, or Ketu
- Weak Moon in the natal chart can increase chances of ocular migraine or visual disturbances

Astrological Remedies:

Moon Remedies:

- Donate milk, rice, or white sweets on Mondays
- Chant: Om Cham Chandrāya Namah – 108 times

Sun Remedies:

- Offer water to the Sun every morning using a copper vessel
- Chant: Om Ghṛṇi Sūryāya Namah – 108 times

Ketu & Rahu Remedies:

- Ketu: Om Kem Ketave Namah – 108 times
- Rahu: Om Bhraam Bhreem Bhraum Sah Rahave Namah – 108 times
- Donate coconut and black sesame seeds in running water
- Feed a black dog

Gemstone Remedies (only after proper horoscope analysis):

- Moon weak: Pearl (Moti)
- Sun weak: Ruby (Manikya)
- Rahu weak: Hessonite (Gomed)
- Ketu weak: Cat's Eye (Lehsunia)

Yogic & Natural Remedies:

Yoga:

- Shavasana – For relaxation and stress relief
- Anulom-Vilom Pranayama – For nervous system purification
- Bhramari Pranayama – To relieve headache and calm the mind

Ayurvedic Support:

- Brahmi and Shankhapushpi – Calm the nerves and reduce headache
- Triphala – Eye cleansing and protection
- Tulsi – Mental clarity and immune support

Natural Precautions:

- Reduce screen time
- Avoid bright or harsh lighting
- Ensure 7–8 hours of sleep daily

Chapter Insight:

Ocular Migraine occurs due to temporary constriction of ocular and cerebral blood vessels, stress, hormonal factors, and planetary influences (Moon, Sun, Rahu, Ketu). Astrological remedies, combined with yoga, Ayurveda, and natural lifestyle adjustments, can help reduce frequency, protect eye health, and maintain mental clarity.

Chapter 11

Mental & Psychological Disorders

(Reserved for future diseases)

Chapter 12

Developmental & Genetic Disorders

(Reserved for future diseases)

Chapter 13

Eye & Vision Disorders

20. Conjunctivitis (Eye Flu / "Aankh Aana") – Medical, Astrological & Holistic Perspective

Introduction

"**Aankh Aana**," commonly known as **Eye Flu** or **Conjunctivitis**, is a highly contagious eye disorder that frequently spreads during the **monsoon and seasonal transition periods**. It affects the conjunctiva—the thin, transparent membrane covering the white part of the eye and the inner surface of the eyelids.

This condition is characterized by **redness, swelling, watering of the eyes, irritation, and discomfort**, and if neglected, it can temporarily impair vision and significantly disturb daily life.

In **Medical Astrology**, eye diseases are not viewed merely as local infections but as manifestations of **planetary affliction, immune sensitivity, emotional imbalance, and seasonal vulnerability**.

To understand conjunctivitis holistically, it must be analyzed through **three integrated lenses**:

1. Medical (Modern Science)
2. Astrological (Vedic Astrology)
3. Preventive and Remedial (Spiritual + Lifestyle)

Medical Perspective (Modern Medical View)

Causes of Conjunctivitis

From a medical standpoint, conjunctivitis can occur due to:

- **Viral infection** (most common and highly contagious)
- **Bacterial infection**

- **Allergic reactions** (dust, pollen, cosmetics)
- **Poor hygiene**, especially touching eyes with contaminated hands
- **Direct contact** with an infected individual
- Use of **contaminated towels, pillows, cosmetics, or eye products**

Monsoon humidity and stagnant water increase viral survival, making outbreaks more common.

Common Symptoms

- Redness and inflammation of the eyes
- Excessive watering or sticky discharge
- Burning or itching sensation
- Eyelids sticking together, especially after sleep
- Sensitivity to light (photophobia)
- Mild blurring of vision (temporary)

Medical Management & Precautions

- Wash eyes gently with **clean, lukewarm water**
- Use **prescribed eye drops** only (avoid self-medication)
- Maintain distance from infected individuals
- Do **not share towels, handkerchiefs, pillow covers, or cosmetics**
- Avoid touching or rubbing the eyes
- Maintain strict personal hygiene

Most viral conjunctivitis resolves within **7–10 days**, but secondary infections require medical supervision.

Astrological Perspective on Eye Flu

In Vedic Astrology, the **eyes are governed by multiple planets and houses**, making eye disorders a sensitive diagnostic indicator of planetary imbalance.

Planets Associated with Eye Disorders

Venus (Shukra)

- Primary significator of **eyes, vision, beauty, and ocular comfort**
- Afflicted Venus can cause:
    - Eye infections
    - Allergic conjunctivitis
    - Watery or irritated eyes

Moon (Chandra)

- Governs **body fluids, immunity, and sensitivity**
- A weak Moon increases:
    - Susceptibility to infections
    - Seasonal and viral eye flu
    - Stress-induced eye strain

Rahu and Ketu

- Cause **sudden, contagious, recurring eye problems**
- Rahu especially triggers **epidemic-type infections**
- Ketu may cause hidden inflammation or slow healing

Relevant Houses for Eye Diseases

- **Lagna (1st House)** – Overall physical health
- **Second House (2nd House)** – Right eye
- **Twelfth House (12th House)** – Left eye

Affliction to these houses by malefics or during adverse **Dasha–Antardasha** periods increases vulnerability to conjunctivitis.

Astrological Remedies for Eye Flu

Strengthening Moon and Venus

- Observe **fasting on Mondays and Fridays** (light, sattvic diet)
- Offer **raw milk mixed with water** to the Moon
- Wear **clean white clothes**, use mild natural fragrances
- Maintain emotional calmness and mental hygiene

Charity and Service Remedies

- Donate **white items** such as rice, milk, sugar to the needy
- Support **eye patients**, eye camps, or distribute prescribed eye drops
- Service related to vision has strong karmic healing effect

Mantra Therapy

- Chant **108 times daily**:
    - *Om Chandraya Namah*
    - *Om Shukraya Namah*

Mantra vibrations help balance fluids, immunity, and ocular sensitivity.

Rahu–Ketu Pacification

- Every Saturday, immerse **blue flowers** in flowing water
- Perform **Rahu–Ketu Shanti Yagya** under guidance of a qualified priest
- Avoid intoxication, excessive screen exposure, and late nights

Preventive Astrological & Lifestyle Guidelines

- Avoid excessive screen time during Rahu-affected periods
- Maintain eye hygiene during Moon-sensitive days
- Avoid touching eyes unnecessarily
- Sleep adequately; eye health is deeply linked with rest
- Keep emotions balanced—anger and stress directly affect vision

Chapter Insight

Conjunctivitis is not just an **external eye infection**, but a combined result of:

- Seasonal vulnerability
- Weak immunity
- Emotional sensitivity
- Planetary imbalance

True prevention and recovery occur when **medical treatment is supported by astrological correction, disciplined hygiene, emotional stability, and sattvic living**.

Medical & Ethical Disclaimer

Eye flu is highly contagious. Medical treatment should never be delayed. Astrological remedies are **supportive measures** and must be practiced **alongside proper medical care**, not as a replacement.

21. Myopia (Near-Sightedness) – A Medical, Astrological, Ayurvedic & Yogic Perspective

Introduction

Myopia, commonly known as **near-sightedness**, is a widespread ocular condition in which a person can see nearby objects clearly, but **distant objects appear blurred or unclear**. This condition has increased significantly in modern times due to excessive screen exposure, reduced outdoor activity, and prolonged near-work.

In holistic health sciences, myopia is not seen merely as a refractive error. Both **Ayurveda and Vedic Medical Astrology** consider it an indicator of **eye muscle strain, nervous sensitivity, mental focus imbalance, and planetary disharmony**.

To understand myopia comprehensively, it must be examined through:

1. Medical Science
2. Vedic Astrology
3. Ayurvedic & Yogic Healing Practices

Medical Perspective (Scientific Viewpoint)

Causes of Myopia

From a modern medical standpoint, myopia occurs due to improper focusing of light on the retina. Common causes include:

- Prolonged use of **mobile phones, computers, tablets, and reading at close distance**
- Continuous strain on **ocular muscles**
- **Genetic predisposition** or family history
- Reduced exposure to natural sunlight
- Improper posture and inadequate eye rest

Medical Management & Preventive Care

- Regular **eye examinations** to track progression
- Use of **prescribed spectacles or contact lenses**
- Following the **20-20-20 rule**:
    - Every 20 minutes, look at something 20 feet away for 20 seconds
- Reducing screen time and avoiding blue-light exposure
- Proper lighting while reading or working

Medical correction improves vision clarity but does not address deeper energetic or constitutional causes.

Astrological Perspective on Myopia

In Vedic Astrology, eyesight is governed by **multiple planets**, each influencing vision from different dimensions.

Planetary Influences on Near-Sightedness

Saturn (Shani)

- Causes **chronic weakness, delayed clarity, and structural issues**
- Afflicted Saturn may lead to:
    - Gradual loss of distant vision
    - Long-term dependence on spectacles

Moon (Chandra)

- Governs **mind, fluids, nerves, and sensitivity**
- An unstable Moon causes:
    - Mental strain affecting eyesight
    - Eye fatigue and fluctuating vision

Rahu

- Represents **artificial environments, screens, illusion, over-stimulation**

- Strongly linked with:
    - Excessive screen use
    - Sudden or progressive vision defects

Sun (Surya)

- Primary significator of **eyesight and visual power**
- A debilitated or afflicted Sun may cause:
    - Reduced eye strength
    - Weak optic vitality

Relevant Houses

- **2nd House** – Right eye
- **12th House** – Left eye
- **Lagna & Lagna Lord** – Overall eye health
- **5th House** – Visual intelligence and perception

Affliction to these houses or their lords often manifests as refractive errors like myopia.

Astrological Remedies for Myopia

Strengthening the Sun (Primary Remedy)

- Offer **water to the rising Sun** every morning
- Chant **11 times daily**:
    - *Om Suryaya Namah*
- Use copper vessels for water storage

This enhances ocular vitality and visual clarity.

Pacifying Rahu

- Chant **108 times** on Wednesday or Saturday:
    - *Om Rahave Namah*

- Reduce screen time during Rahu Mahadasha / Antardasha
- Avoid late-night digital exposure

Saturn Remedies

- On Saturdays:
  - Offer water to the **Peepal tree**
  - Light a mustard oil lamp
- Maintain discipline and routine in lifestyle

Ayurvedic-Astrological Support

- **Triphala therapy**:
  - Soak Triphala powder overnight
  - Strain and gently wash eyes in the morning
- This balances Pitta and strengthens optic nerves

(Always maintain hygiene and consult an expert before eye application)

Gemstone Guidance

- If the **Sun is weak**, a **Ruby (Manikya)** may be recommended
- **Gemstones must ONLY be worn after full horoscope analysis**
  Improper gemstone use may worsen symptoms.

Yoga & Yogic Eye Therapy

Trataka Meditation

- Focus steadily on a candle flame without blinking
- Strengthens eye muscles and optic nerves
- Improves concentration and visual endurance

Eye Exercises

- Palming: warming eyes with palms
- Blinking exercises
- Circular eye movements

Eye Cleansing

- Splash eyes with **cool, clean water**
- Practice Netra Snana (eye washing) under guidance

Mantra for Eye Health

Daily chanting strengthens ocular energy and solar vitality:

Mantra:

Om Namo Bhagavate Suryaya Adityaya
Akshi Tejah Pradaya Namah

- Chant **11 or 108 times daily**
- Best practiced at sunrise

Holistic Insight

Myopia reflects:

- Excessive inward focus
- Over-dependence on artificial environments
- Weak solar energy and mental strain

True improvement lies in **combining medical correction with planetary balancing, Ayurvedic nourishment, yogic discipline, and lifestyle correction**.

Medical & Ethical Disclaimer

Myopia requires regular ophthalmological monitoring. Astrological, Ayurvedic, and yogic remedies are **supportive practices**, not replacements for medical treatment.

22. Hyperopia (Farsightedness) – An Integrated Astrological, Ayurvedic & Yogic Perspective

Introduction

Hyperopia, or farsightedness, is a visual disorder in which distant objects are seen clearly, but near objects appear blurred. While often mild in children, it may persist into adulthood. From an integrative perspective, Hyperopia is not only due to anatomical factors of the eye, but also reflects subtle energy imbalances and planetary influences that affect visual acuity.

Medical Astrology, Ayurveda, and Yoga together help in understanding why certain individuals develop farsightedness, how planetary periods influence vision, and what preventive and supportive measures can be adopted.

Common Causes of Hyperopia (Medical & Lifestyle Factors)

From a medical viewpoint, Hyperopia may be triggered by:

- Shortened eyeball (axial length less than normal)
- Reduced lens power or flexibility
- Genetic predisposition
  While these factors explain the structural cause, they do not fully account for progression, eye strain, or discomfort, which are better understood through astrology and holistic care.

Astrological Causes of Hyperopia

According to Vedic Medical Astrology, farsightedness is primarily associated with disturbances in Jupiter (Guru), along with the influence of Sun (Surya) and Venus (Shukra).

Key Planetary Indications

- **Jupiter (Guru):** Governs wisdom and eye function; imbalance can reduce visual sharpness

- **Sun (Surya):** Primary source of eye energy; weak Sun can manifest as refractive errors
- **Venus (Shukra):** Associated with vision and aesthetics; debilitated Venus may contribute to eye problems

Astrological Combinations Indicating Susceptibility

- Weak or afflicted Jupiter in natal chart
- Sun afflicted by malefic planets or in unfavorable houses
- Venus debilitated or in conjunction with malefics
  Such planetary conditions may manifest as farsightedness, eye strain, or difficulty focusing on near objects, particularly during adverse planetary dashas and transits.

Ayurvedic Perspective on Hyperopia

In Ayurveda, Hyperopia is often linked to **Vata imbalance**, with secondary **Pitta** involvement affecting ocular energy.

Dosha Involvement

- **Vata:** Causes eye strain, difficulty focusing, dryness, and nervous tension in ocular muscles
- **Pitta:** Governs vision; imbalance can weaken retinal function and clarity

Contributing Ayurvedic Factors

- Weak digestive fire (Mandagni) affecting nutrient absorption for eyes
- Excessive exposure to bright light or digital screens
- Improper rest and eye overuse
  Ayurveda emphasizes diet, eye exercises, and herbal remedies to strengthen ocular function and maintain visual balance.

Yogic Support for Hyperopia

Yoga improves eye flexibility, strengthens ocular muscles, enhances circulation, and balances nervous system activity.

Recommended Yogic Practices (to be practiced gently)

Pranayama

- **Anulom Vilom:** Balances energy flow affecting eyes
- **Bhramari:** Reduces eye stress and mental tension

Asanas

- **Trataka (fixed gazing):** Improves focus and near vision
- **Tadasana and Bhujangasana:** Enhance blood flow to eyes
- Gentle **palming and blinking exercises** for ocular relaxation

Meditation

- Reduces eye strain caused by stress
- Supports recovery during unfavorable planetary periods

Yoga acts as a preventive and supportive practice, not a replacement for optical correction or medical treatment.

Astrological & Spiritual Remedies

Planetary Remedies

1. **Strengthening Jupiter (Guru):**
   - Chant Om Brim Brihaspataye Namah regularly
   - Offer yellow-colored items on Thursday
2. **Strengthening Sun (Surya):**
   - Morning sun worship with water offering
   - Chant Om Ghṛṇi Sūryāya Namah (11 or 108 times)
3. **Strengthening Venus (Shukra):**
   - Chant Om Draam Dreem Draum Sah Shukraya Namah
   - Offer white flowers or sweets on Friday

These remedies should be practiced with faith, consistency, and ethical intent.

Home-Based Ayurvedic Remedies

1. **Triphala Eye Drops:** Improves vision and eye health
2. **Honey and Triphala Mixture:** Taken under guidance to enhance ocular strength
3. **Cold water or rosewater compresses:** Relieves eye strain
4. **Dietary support:** Include vitamin A, beta-carotene, and antioxidants

Preventive Guidelines

- Maintain proper screen and reading distance
- Avoid eye overstrain and prolonged digital exposure
- Regularly practice eye exercises, palming, and Trataka
- Observe preventive care during adverse Jupiter, Sun, or Venus periods

Ethical Note

The remedies and practices mentioned here are supportive in nature and should always complement, not replace, professional eye care or optical correction.

Chapter Insight

Hyperopia reflects a combination of structural eye factors, Vata-Pitta imbalance, and subtle planetary influences (Jupiter, Sun, Venus). An integrated approach using Astrology, Ayurveda, and Yoga provides preventive strategies, eye-strengthening exercises, and planetary remedies for long-term visual health.

23. Astigmatism – An Integrated Astrological, Ayurvedic & Yogic Perspective

Introduction

Astigmatism is a visual disorder in which vision appears blurred or distorted at all distances due to an irregular curvature of the cornea or lens. This prevents light rays from focusing evenly on the retina. While it may occur alone, it is sometimes associated with Hyperopia (farsightedness) or Myopia (nearsightedness).

Medical Astrology, Ayurveda, and Yoga together help in understanding why certain individuals develop astigmatism, how planetary influences affect visual stability, and what supportive and preventive measures can be adopted.

Common Causes of Astigmatism (Medical & Lifestyle Factors)

Medical Factors:

- Irregular curvature of cornea or lens from birth
- Eye injury or post-surgical changes
- Genetic inheritance
- Sometimes occurs alongside Hyperopia or Myopia

Symptoms :

- Blurred or distorted vision
- Headaches
- Eye strain and fatigue
- Difficulty seeing at night

Medical Treatments :

- Cylindrical lens glasses or contact lenses
- LASIK or PRK laser surgery
- Regular eye check-ups

Astrological Causes of Astigmatism

According to Vedic Medical Astrology, astigmatism is influenced by Rahu, Ketu, Saturn (Shani), Moon, Mercury (Budh), Sun (Surya), and Venus (Shukra).

Key Planetary Indications:

- **Rahu and Ketu:** Influence vision distortion; especially when affecting 2nd, 12th, or Lagna houses
- **Saturn (Shani):** Slows vision, contributes to eye fatigue and chronic strain
- **Moon (Chandra) or Mercury (Budh):** Afflicted by malefics can disturb neuro-visual communication
- **Sun (Surya) or Venus (Shukra):** Debilitated or afflicted by malefics can cause eye defects

Indicative Horoscope Patterns :

- Rahu/Ketu in key houses (2nd, 12th, Lagna)
- Afflicted Moon or Mercury
- Sun or Venus debilitated or under malefic influence
  Such planetary conditions may manifest as distorted vision, blurred images, headaches, or eye strain, particularly during adverse Dasha and transit periods.

Ayurvedic Perspective on Astigmatism

Dosha Imbalance:

- **Vata:** Eye strain, tension, dryness, and irregular focus
- **Pitta:** Governs vision and retinal function; imbalance can reduce visual clarity

Contributing Ayurvedic Factors:

- Weak digestive fire (Mandagni) affecting ocular nutrition
- Excessive screen or reading strain
- Improper rest and eye fatigue

Ayurvedic Advice:

- Eye-strengthening exercises and relaxation
- Herbal support (Triphala, honey)
- Diet rich in antioxidants and vitamin A

Yogic Support for Astigmatism

Recommended Practices (to be practiced gently):

Pranayama:

- **Bhastrika:** Clears ocular strain and enhances circulation
- **Anulom-Vilom:** Balances energy and supports neuro-visual function

Asanas & Eye Exercises:

- **Trataka (fixed gazing on flame or point):** Improves focus and eye coordination
- **Sheetali Pranayama & Brahma Mudra:** Relax eyes and mind
- Gentle palming, blinking, and ocular rotations

Meditation:

- Reduces stress, which otherwise exacerbates eye fatigue
- Supports recovery during adverse planetary periods

Astrological & Spiritual Remedies

Sun & Eye Health:

- Offer morning water (Arghya) to Sun
- Chant: Om Ghṛṇi Sūryāya Namah

Rahu & Ketu Pacification:

- Chant: Om Bhraam Bhreem Bhraum Sah Rahave Namah (for Rahu)
- Chant: Om Kem Ketave Namah (for Ketu)

Recommended 108 times every Saturday

Other Practices:

- Trataka (focused gazing)
- Regular Gayatri mantra chanting
- Neem leaves consumption or rosewater in eye rinse (with medical guidance)
- Saturn pacification: Worship Peepal tree, light mustard oil lamp on Saturday

Gemstone Remedies

- **Weak Sun:** Ruby (Manikya)
- **Weak Venus:** Diamond, Opal, or Venus-related stones

Only after careful horoscope analysis

Home-Based Ayurvedic & Yogic Practices

- Eye exercises: palming, blinking, and gentle rotations
- Pranayama: Bhastrika and Anulom-Vilom
- Eye-strengthening asanas: Trataka, Sheetali, Brahma Mudra
- Triphala powder with honey (under Ayurvedic guidance)
- Regular eye hygiene with cold water or rosewater

Preventive Guidelines

- Avoid prolonged screen or reading strain
- Maintain proper lighting and distance while reading
- Take regular eye breaks and rest
- Observe planetary remedies during adverse Rahu, Ketu, or Saturn periods

Ethical Note

The practices and remedies mentioned are supportive in nature and should **complement**, not replace, professional ophthalmological care.

Chapter Insight

Astigmatism results from a combination of corneal/lens irregularities, Vata-Pitta imbalance, and adverse planetary influences (Rahu, Ketu, Shani, Sun, Venus). Integrating Astrology, Ayurveda, and Yoga offers preventive measures, vision-strengthening exercises, and planetary remedies for maintaining long-term ocular health.

24. Presbyopia – An Integrated Astrological, Ayurvedic & Yogic Perspective

Introduction

Presbyopia is an age-related visual disorder in which near vision becomes difficult, affecting activities such as reading, sewing, or mobile phone use. It typically begins after the age of 40.

Medical Astrology, Ayurveda, and Yoga together help understand why vision weakens with age, how planetary influences affect ocular function, and what supportive measures can improve near-vision clarity.

Common Causes of Presbyopia (Medical & Lifestyle Factors)

Medical Causes:

- Decreased flexibility of the eye lens
- Weakening of ocular muscles
- Difficulty focusing on near objects

Symptoms / लक्षण:

- Need to hold books or mobile devices at arm's length
- Eye strain and headaches
- Difficulty seeing in low-light conditions

Medical Treatments :

- Reading glasses
- Bifocal or progressive lenses
- Contact lenses or surgical options (Monovision LASIK)

Astrological Causes of Presbyopia

According to Vedic Medical Astrology, presbyopia is influenced by Sun, Moon, Saturn, Mercury, and Venus, along with key houses related to eyes and aging.

Key Planetary Indications:

- **Sun and Moon:** Weakness reduces visual strength
- **Saturn (Shani):** Associated with aging; slows ocular function over time
- **Mercury and Venus:** Weak or afflicted positions interfere with near vision

Indicative Horoscope Patterns :

- Afflicted Sun or Moon
- Saturn influencing longevity and aging houses
- Disturbances in 2nd house (eyes) and 8th house (age/elderly) Such planetary influences may result in difficulty focusing on near objects, eye strain, and reduced near-vision clarity during adverse Dasha and transit periods.

Ayurvedic Perspective on Presbyopia

Dosha Imbalance:

- **Vata:** Weakens eye coordination and focusing ability
- **Pitta:** Governs eye energy; imbalance reduces clarity

Contributing Ayurvedic Factors:

- Aging naturally reduces eye lens elasticity
- Accumulated eye strain and reduced nourishment
- Weak digestive fire (Mandagni) affecting ocular health

Ayurvedic Advice:

- Eye-strengthening exercises
- Consumption of Triphala and other eye-nourishing herbs
- Diet rich in antioxidants and vitamins for ocular support

Yogic Support for Presbyopia

Recommended Practices (gently and regularly):

Pranayama:

- Anulom-Vilom – balances ocular energy

- Kapalbhati – improves circulation and eye focus
- Sheetali – cools and relaxes eyes

Eye Exercises:

- Up-down and side-to-side eye movements
- Blinking and palming
- Trataka (focused gazing) to strengthen near vision

Meditation:

- Reduces stress, which exacerbates age-related eye strain
- Supports ocular endurance during adverse planetary periods

Eye Hygiene:

- Wash eyes with Triphala water
- Cold compresses or rosewater for relaxation

Astrological & Spiritual Remedies

Sun Remedies:

- Offer water (Arghya) to Sun in the morning
- Chant: Om Ghṛṇi Sūryāya Namah (11 or 108 times daily)

Moon Remedies:

- Chant: Om Cham Chandrāya Namah on Monday 108 times

Saturn Remedies (aging & ocular health):

- Worship Peepal tree on Saturday
- Donate black sesame seeds, mustard oil, and iron

Other Practices:

- Trataka meditation for eye focus
- Regular Gayatri mantra chanting for mental and ocular strength
- Triphala consumption for eye purification

Gemstone Remedies

- **Weak Sun:** Ruby (Manikya)
- **Weak Moon:** Pearl (Moti)

Only after horoscope analysis

Home-Based Ayurvedic & Yogic Practices

- Eye exercises: palming, blinking, up-down & side-to-side movements
- Pranayama: Anulom-Vilom, Kapalbhati, Sheetali
- Eye cleansing with Triphala water
- Cold compress or rosewater application for relaxation

Preventive Guidelines

- Avoid excessive near work without breaks
- Maintain proper lighting and posture while reading or using devices
- Practice regular eye exercises and relaxation
- Follow planetary remedies during adverse Sun, Moon, or Saturn periods

Ethical Note

These remedies and practices are supportive and should **complement**, not replace, professional ophthalmological care.

Chapter Insight

Presbyopia reflects age-related weakening of lens flexibility and ocular muscles, Vata-Pitta imbalance, and planetary influences (Sun, Moon, Saturn, Mercury, Venus). An integrated approach using Astrology, Ayurveda, and Yoga provides eye-strengthening techniques, preventive care, and spiritual remedies to support long-term near-vision health.

25. Cataracts – An Integrated Astrological, Ayurvedic & Yogic Perspective

Introduction

Cataracts is a common eye disorder in which the lens becomes cloudy, giving the impression of looking through a foggy screen. It usually occurs in older age, but may also develop due to diabetes, eye injury, or early aging in some individuals.

Medical Astrology, Ayurveda, and Yoga together help explain why cataracts develop, how planetary influences affect lens clarity, and what supportive and preventive measures can be adopted.

Common Causes of Cataracts (Medical & Lifestyle Factors)

Medical Factors:

- Age-related changes in lens protein structure
- Diabetes, smoking, excessive sun exposure
- Genetic predisposition
- Long-term steroid use
- Eye injury or infection

Symptoms :

- Cloudy, blurred, or foggy vision
- Difficulty seeing at night
- Glare from bright light
- Colors appearing faded

Medical Treatments :

- Early-stage: corrective glasses may help
- Definitive treatment: lens replacement surgery (Cataract Surgery) – safe and commonly performed

Astrological Causes of Cataracts

According to Vedic Medical Astrology, cataracts may be associated with Sun, Saturn, and Ketu, along with the 2nd (eyes) and 12th houses.

Key Planetary Indications:

- Sun (Surya): Governs vision; debilitated or afflicted Sun reduces ocular clarity
- Saturn (Shani): Associated with aging and chronic ocular conditions
- Ketu: Causes vision confusion, foggy eyesight, and mysterious eye disorders

Indicative Horoscope Patterns :

- Malefic influence on Sun in the horoscope
- Ketu or Saturn affecting 2nd or 12th house
- Combination of Sun debilitated and Ketu affliction

Ayurvedic Perspective on Cataracts

Dosha Imbalance:

- Pitta: Governs lens clarity and visual energy; imbalance can cloud vision
- Vata: Contributes to chronic degenerative changes

Contributing Factors:

- Aging process naturally affects lens transparency
- Metabolic issues (like diabetes) accelerate lens clouding
- Environmental stressors such as UV exposure and oxidative stress

Ayurvedic Advice:

- Eye-strengthening herbs and routines (Triphala)
- Balanced diet with antioxidants
- Eye relaxation exercises

Yogic Support for Cataracts

Recommended Practices (gently and regularly):

Pranayama:

- Sheetali – cools and relaxes eyes
- Gentle breathing exercises for ocular circulation

Eye Exercises:

- Trataka (focused gazing) to improve concentration
- Palming and blinking for eye muscle relaxation

Ayurvedic Eye Care:

- Triphala powder soaked overnight, strained, and used to wash eyes (with medical guidance)
- Cold compresses with rosewater or cucumber juice

Astrological & Spiritual Remedies

Sun Remedies:

- Offer water (Arghya) to Sun every morning
- Chant: Om Ghṛṇi Sūryāya Namah (108 times)

Ketu Remedies:

- Chant: Om Kem Ketave Namah on Tuesday or Saturday (108 times)
- Feed a black dog for pacifying Ketu influence

Saturn Remedies:

- Worship Peepal tree on Saturday
- Donate black sesame seeds, mustard oil, and iron

Other Practices:

- Gayatri mantra chanting for eye strength and mental clarity
- Trataka meditation for focused vision

Gemstone Remedies

- Sun weak: Ruby (Manikya)
- Ketu weak: Hessonite (Gomed)

Only after careful horoscope analysis

Preventive Ayurvedic & Yogic Practices

- Eye exercises and gentle palming
- Trataka meditation for visual focus
- Triphala eye wash and cool compresses
- Protective measures from UV exposure

Chapter Insight

Cataracts results from age-related lens changes, Pitta-Vata imbalance, and planetary influences (Sun, Ketu, Saturn). Integrating Astrology, Ayurveda, and Yoga supports lens health, slows visual deterioration, and provides spiritual remedies for maintaining clarity of vision.

26. Glaucoma – An Integrated Astrological, Ayurvedic & Yogic Perspective

Introduction

Glaucoma is a serious eye disorder characterized by increased intraocular pressure (IOP), which can damage the optic nerve and gradually lead to blindness. Often, early-stage glaucoma is asymptomatic, making early detection crucial.

Medical Astrology, Ayurveda, and Yoga together help understand why certain individuals are predisposed to glaucoma, how planetary influences affect ocular pressure and optic nerve health, and what preventive and supportive measures can be applied.

Types & Causes of Glaucoma (Medical & Lifestyle Factors)

Types:

1. Open-Angle Glaucoma: Most common; gradual peripheral vision loss
2. Angle-Closure Glaucoma: Sudden onset; medical emergency
3. Normal-Tension Glaucoma: Optic nerve damage despite normal IOP
4. Congenital Glaucoma: Present from birth
5. Secondary Glaucoma: Due to other diseases or injuries

Symptoms :

- Gradual peripheral vision loss
- Eye pain, redness, nausea (in acute cases)
- Halos around lights
- Difficulty seeing in the dark

Causes :

- Genetic predisposition
- Diabetes, high blood pressure

- Prolonged corticosteroid use
- Eye injury or surgery

Medical Treatments :

- IOP-lowering eye drops
- Laser therapy
- Surgery (Trabeculectomy, drainage implants)
- Early detection is the most effective preventive measure

Astrological Causes of Glaucoma

According to Vedic Medical Astrology, glaucoma is influenced by Saturn, Ketu, Sun, and Mercury, as well as 2nd (eyes) and 12th houses (hidden, chronic conditions).

Key Planetary Indications:

- Saturn (Shani): Chronic, age-related, or complex ocular disorders
- Ketu: Blindness, confusion, mysterious eye ailments
- Sun (Surya): Governs vision; afflicted or debilitated Sun can cause weakness in eyesight
- Mercury (Budh): Controls neural and visual coordination

Indicative Horoscope Patterns :

- Afflicted Sun or Ketu
- Saturn aspecting or influencing 2nd or 12th house
- Combination of malefic influence on vision-related houses

Ayurvedic Perspective on Glaucoma

Dosha Imbalance:

- Vata: Contributes to optic nerve degeneration and chronic vision issues

- Pitta: Governs eye energy; imbalance can increase IOP and visual strain

Contributing Ayurvedic Factors:

- Aging and degeneration of ocular structures
- Metabolic disturbances like diabetes
- Environmental and lifestyle stressors

Ayurvedic Advice:

- Triphala decoction for eye wash (with guidance)
- Eye relaxation and cooling practices
- Balanced diet and antioxidants to support ocular health

Yogic Support for Glaucoma

Recommended Practices (gently and under guidance):

Pranayama:

- Anulom-Vilom – balances energy and reduces ocular strain
- Kapalbhati (gentle, slow) – improves ocular circulation

Eye Exercises:

- Trataka (focused gazing) to strengthen vision and concentration
- Palming and gentle eye movements

Ayurvedic Eye Care:

- Triphala decoction for eye wash (consult physician)
- Cool compress with rosewater or cucumber juice

Astrological & Spiritual Remedies

Sun Remedies:

- Offer water to Sun daily
- Chant: Om Ghr̥ṇi Sūryāya Namah (11 or 108 times)

Ketu Remedies:

- Chant: Om Kem Ketave Namah on Tuesday or Saturday (108 times)
- Feed a black dog or perform Ketu puja with lamp/incense

Saturn Remedies:

- Circumambulate a Peepal tree on Saturday
- Light mustard oil lamp and chant: Om Sham Shanaiścharāya Namah

Other Supportive Mantras:

- Tryambakam (Mahamrityunjaya) mantra – enhances vitality and prevents disease

Gemstone Remedies

- Sun weak: Ruby (Manikya)
- Ketu weak: Hessonite (Gomed)

Only after careful horoscope analysis

Preventive Ayurvedic & Yogic Practices

- Eye exercises and Trataka for optic nerve strength
- Pranayama (Anulom-Vilom, gentle Kapalbhati)
- Triphala eye wash and cooling applications with rosewater or cucumber

Chapter Insight

Glaucoma is a chronic, potentially blinding disorder caused by elevated intraocular pressure, metabolic stress, Vata-Pitta imbalance, and planetary influences (Saturn, Ketu, Sun). An integrated approach using Astrology, Ayurveda, and Yoga provides preventive care, optic nerve support, and spiritual remedies to slow progression and maintain vision.

27. Macular Degeneration – An Integrated Astrological, Ayurvedic & Yogic Perspective

Introduction

Macular Degeneration is an eye disorder in which the central part of the retina (macula) gets damaged, leading to blurred or distorted central vision. It is especially common with aging and is therefore also called Age-related Macular Degeneration (AMD).

Medical Astrology, Ayurveda, and Yoga together help understand the susceptibility, preventive measures, and supportive remedies for maintaining central vision, slowing progression, and improving overall ocular health.

Types & Medical Causes of Macular Degeneration

Types:

1. Dry AMD (≈90%) – Slowly develops; yellow deposits (drusen) appear in the retina
2. Wet AMD (≈10%) – Rapid central vision loss; abnormal blood vessels form under the retina

Symptoms :

- Blurred central vision or blind spots
- Difficulty recognizing faces
- Wavy or distorted lines
- Reduced color perception

Risk Factors :

- Age 60+ and genetic predisposition
- Smoking, obesity, high blood pressure
- Excessive exposure to sunlight

Medical Treatment :

- Dry AMD: Nutrition (zinc, vitamins A, C, E), lifestyle management
- Wet AMD: Anti-VEGF injections, laser therapy
- Complete cure may not be possible, but management and preventive care are highly effective

Astrological Causes of Macular Degeneration

Relevant Planets & Houses:

- Sun (Surya): Governs vision and light perception
- Venus (Shukra): Governs eye clarity and beauty
- Saturn (Shani): Linked to aging and degeneration
- Ketu: Associated with confusion, darkness, and distortion
- 2nd House & 12th House: Eye-related houses

Astrological combinations that increase susceptibility include Sun or Venus in conjunction with malefics like Saturn or Ketu, or afflicted 2nd/12th house.

Astrological Remedies

Sun Remedies:

- Offer red flowers in water to the Sun daily
- Chant: Om Ghṛṇi Sūryāya Namah– 108 times

Venus Remedies:

- On Fridays, donate white cloth, rice, and curd
- Chant: ॐ शुक्राय नमः – 108 times

Ketu Remedies:

- Chant: Om Kem Ketave Namah on Tuesday or Saturday – 108 times

- Feed a black dog with bread

Saturn Remedies:

- Worship Peepal tree on Saturdays
- Donate iron
- Chant: Om Praam Preem Praum Sah Shanicharaya Namah– 108 times

Gemstone Remedies

- Sun weak: Ruby (Manikya)
- Venus weak: Diamond or Opal
- Ketu weak: Hessonite (Gomed)

Gemstones should be chosen only after careful horoscope analysis.

Yogic & Ayurvedic Support

- Trataka meditation: Focus on a single point to strengthen vision
- Triphala powder: Internal use and eye washes for ocular cleansing
- Ayurvedic eye formulations (Netra Sanjeevani): As per practitioner guidance
- Pranayama: Especially Anulom-Vilom and Bhramari to improve circulation and eye function
- Cooling eye treatments: Rosewater compresses or cold packs

Chapter Insight

Macular Degeneration, particularly age-related, results from retinal degeneration, lifestyle factors, genetic predisposition, and planetary influences (Sun, Venus, Saturn, Ketu). An integrated approach combining Astrology, Ayurveda, and Yoga supports central vision, reduces progression, and enhances overall ocular health.

28. Dry Eye Syndrome – An Integrated Astrological, Ayurvedic & Yogic Perspective

Introduction

Dry Eye Syndrome is a common but uncomfortable eye condition in which the eyes do not produce sufficient or good-quality tears. This can lead to burning, stinging, itching, heaviness, and sometimes blurred vision. If left untreated, it may damage the cornea. An integrated approach combining Medical, Astrological, Ayurvedic, and Yogic insights helps in understanding causes, preventive measures, and supportive remedies.

Medical Perspective

Symptoms:

- Burning or stinging in the eyes
- Foreign body sensation ("something in the eye")
- Redness and itching
- Reflex tearing when eyes dry
- Blurred vision, especially while reading or using screens

Primary Causes:

- Aging, particularly after 50 years
- Prolonged screen exposure (reduced blinking)
- Environmental factors (AC, dust, sunlight, pollution)
- Certain medications (Antihistamines, Antidepressants)
- Hormonal changes, especially in women
- Autoimmune disorders like Sjögren's Syndrome

Treatment:

- Artificial tears (eye drops)
- Omega-3 supplements

- Use of humidifiers
- Eye hygiene and warm compress
- Severe cases: punctal plugs or medications

Astrological Perspective

Key Planets & Houses:

- Sun (Surya) – Governs vision, eye clarity, and dryness
- Venus (Shukra) – Maintains body and eye moisture
- Ketu – Shadow, subtle disturbances
- Saturn (Shani) – Vata (dryness), chronic conditions
- 12th House – Eye-related discomfort

Astrological Combinations Indicating Susceptibility:

- Weak Sun and Venus with malefic aspect from Shani or Ketu can lead to dryness, reduced vision clarity, or persistent burning in eyes

Astrological Remedies:

Sun Remedies:

- Offer water to the Sun every morning using a copper vessel
- Chant: Om Ghṛṇi Sūryāya Namah – 108 times

Venus Remedies:

- Donate rice, white clothes, or curd on Fridays
- Chant: Om Draam Dreem Draum Sah Shukraya Namah – 108 times

Ketu Remedies:

- Chant: Om Kem Ketave Namah– 108 times
- Feed a black dog
- Immerse coconut in running water on Tuesday or Saturday

Saturn Remedies:

- Light a mustard oil lamp under a Peepal tree on Saturday
- Chant: ॐ शं शनैश्चराय नमः – 108 times

Gemstone Remedies (after proper horoscope analysis):

- Venus weak: Diamond or Opal
- Sun weak: Ruby (Manikya)
- Ketu weak: Hessonite (Gomed)

Yogic & Ayurvedic Support

Yoga Practices:

- Trataka meditation – For eye focus and moisture retention
- Sheetali and Sheetkari Pranayama – Increases body and eye cooling/moisture

Ayurvedic Remedies:

- Eye wash with Triphala water – Cleansing and rejuvenation
- 1–2 drops of ghee (or medicated sesame oil) in eyes as per Ayurvedic guidance
- Anjan (traditional Ayurvedic eye application)

Dietary Recommendations:

- Omega-3 rich foods: flaxseeds, walnuts
- Foods rich in vitamins A, C, E
- Adequate water intake

Chapter Insight:

Dry Eye Syndrome occurs due to aging, environmental factors, hormonal changes, and planetary influences (Sun, Venus, Saturn, Ketu). A combination of astrological remedies, yoga, Ayurveda, and dietary/lifestyle adjustments helps restore eye moisture, reduce irritation, and maintain overall ocular health.

Chapter 14

Reproductive & Gynecological Disorders

29. Breast Cancer – An Integrated Astrological, Ayurvedic & Yogic Perspective

(Note: Always seek proper medical diagnosis and treatment; astrology provides supplementary spiritual and psychological support only.)

Medical Perspective

Symptoms:

- Lump or thickening in the breast or underarm
- Change in breast size, shape, or skin texture
- Nipple discharge or inversion
- Persistent pain or swelling
- Unexplained weight loss, fatigue (in advanced stages)

Primary Causes:

- Genetic mutations (BRCA1 / BRCA2)
- Hormonal imbalance (estrogen dominance)
- Family history and hereditary factors
- Lifestyle factors (stress, obesity, unhealthy diet)
- Environmental toxins and radiation exposure

Astrological Perspective

In Vedic astrology, breast-related diseases are strongly connected with emotional imbalance, hormonal disturbances, and afflicted watery planets.

Key Planets & Houses:

- **4th House:** Chest, heart, breasts
- **6th House:** Disease and illness
- **8th House:** Chronic illness, surgery, life-threatening disease
- **12th House:** Hospitalization, loss of vitality

Planetary Influences:
- **Moon:** Breasts, fluids, emotional health (most critical)
- **Venus:** Female reproductive system, hormones
- **Mars:** Surgery, inflammation, malignancy
- **Rahu / Ketu:** Hidden, karmic, or sudden diseases

Astrological Combinations Indicating Susceptibility:

- Malefic planets (Saturn, Mars, Rahu, Ketu) influencing the **4th house or Moon**
- Afflicted **Moon or Venus** in the 4th, 6th, 8th, or 12th house
- **Rahu + Moon (Chandra Grahan Yoga)**
- **Saturn + Moon (Vish Yoga)**
- Venus under severe malefic aspect, especially in female charts

Astrological Remedies

(Supportive in nature; not a substitute for medical treatment)

Mantras & Chanting:

- **Mahamrityunjaya Mantra** – For healing and protection:

Om Tryambakam Yajamahe
Sugandhim Pushtivardhanam
Urvarukamiva Bandhanan
Mrityor Mukshiya Maamritat → Chant **108 times daily**, preferably during **Brahma Muhurat**

- **Durga Saptashati (Devi Path)** – For feminine strength and protection

Gemstone Remedies

(Only after proper horoscope analysis)

• Weak Moon → **Pearl (Moti)** in silver
• Afflicted Venus → **Diamond or White Sapphire** (only in suitable charts)

Yogic & Ayurvedic Support

- Gentle **pranayama** (Anulom–Vilom, Bhramari) under guidance
- Meditation and mantra-based healing
- Ayurvedic support as complementary therapy (doctor-guided)

Dietary Recommendations:

- Light, sattvic, hormone-balancing diet
- Fresh fruits, vegetables, and adequate hydration
- Avoid excess sugar, processed food, and toxins

Chapter Insight:

• Breast cancer reflects a **deep link between emotional stress, hormonal imbalance, and lunar afflictions**
• Astrology helps identify **karmic and psychological vulnerability**, while medicine treats the physical condition
• True healing requires **medical care + emotional balance + spiritual strength**

30. Prostate Cancer– An Integrated Astrological, Ayurvedic & Yogic Perspective

(Note: Proper medical diagnosis and treatment are mandatory. Astrology offers supplementary, spiritual, and karmic insight — not a replacement for medical care.)

Medical Perspective

Symptoms:

- Frequent urination, especially at night
- Difficulty or pain during urination
- Weak or interrupted urine flow
- Blood in urine or semen
- Pain in lower back, hips, or thighs
- Reduced sexual desire or erectile issues

Primary Causes:

- Increasing age (risk rises after 50 years)
- Genetic / family history
- Hormonal imbalance (testosterone-related)
- High-fat diet, processed meat, smoking
- Obesity and physical inactivity

Medical Diagnosis & Treatment:

- PSA Test (Prostate Specific Antigen)
- MRI, Ultrasound, Biopsy
- Treatment options:

- Surgery (Prostatectomy)
- Radiation Therapy
- Hormone Therapy
- Immunotherapy

Ayurvedic Support (Complementary):

• Varun, Gokshura, Punarnava
• Shilajit, Shwet Musli, Ashwagandha
• Giloy for immunity
(Use strictly under expert supervision)

Astrological Perspective

Prostate cancer relates to **reproductive organs, urinary system, glandular growth, and chronic karmic disease**.

Key Planets & Houses:

Key Planets:
• **Venus:** Male reproductive organs, urinary and hormonal system
• **Mars:** Glands, blood circulation, inflammation
• **Saturn:** Chronic diseases, cancerous growth
• **Rahu:** Toxicity, abnormal cell multiplication

Key Houses:
• **8th House:** Hidden, chronic diseases, surgery
• **12th House:** Hospitalization, loss of vitality
• **6th House:** Disease and illness

Astrological Combinations Indicating Susceptibility:

• Debilitated or afflicted **Venus** (with Saturn or Rahu)
• **Rahu / Ketu / Saturn** placed in the 8th house
• **Saturn + Rahu** conjunction (strong chronic disease yoga)
• Venus–Mars affliction in the 12th house
• Afflicted **Scorpio or Cancer signs**, increasing risk of secret or reproductive disorders

Astrological Remedies

(Supportive, spiritual, and preventive in nature)

Mantra Remedies:

Saturn Mantra (for chronic disease relief):
Om Praam Preem Praum Sah Shanicharaya Namah
→ Chant **108 times on Saturdays**

Venus Mantra (reproductive & hormonal health):
Om Draam Dreem Draum Sah Shukraya Namah

→ Chant **108 times on Fridays**

Rahu Beej Mantra (to reduce toxic influence):
Om Bhraam Bhreem Bhraum Sah Rahave Namah

→ Chant **108 times on Wednesday / Saturdays**

Natural & Lifestyle Remedies:

- Offer water to the **Sun** daily using a copper vessel
- Consume **Neem & Giloy decoction** regularly
- Offer water at the **Peepal tree** on Saturdays
- Maintain sexual discipline and sattvic lifestyle

Gemstone Remedies

(Only after proper horoscope analysis)

- **Blue Sapphire (Neelam):** If Saturn is benefic
- **Opal / Diamond:** To strengthen Venus

Incorrect gemstones may worsen disease — **chart verification is mandatory**

Yogic & Ayurvedic Support

- Gentle yoga under medical guidance
- Pranayama (regulated breathing)
- Stress reduction through meditation

Dietary Recommendations:

- Low-fat, plant-based diet
- Avoid processed meat, alcohol, smoking

- Increase fruits, vegetables, hydration
- Maintain healthy weight

Charity & Seva (Highly Recommended):

- Donate oil, black clothes, iron, or urad dal on Saturdays
- Offer medicines or fruits silently to patients
- Donate white clothes or rice on Fridays

Chapter Insight:

- Prostate cancer reflects **Venus–Saturn–Rahu imbalance** at physical and karmic levels
- Early stages often remain hidden — astrology highlights **latent disease patterns**
- Medical treatment addresses the body; astrology supports **mental strength, discipline, and karmic balance**
- Remedies work best when combined with **timely diagnosis, disciplined lifestyle, and spiritual alignment**

31. Cervical Cancer (Cancer of the Cervix– An Integrated Astrological, Ayurvedic & Yogic Perspective

Medical Perspective

Cervical cancer develops in the cervix, the lower part of the uterus connecting to the vagina. It is primarily caused by persistent infection with high-risk strains of Human Papillomavirus (HPV). Early detection through screening (Pap smear, HPV test) significantly improves outcomes. Medical management includes surgery, radiotherapy, chemotherapy, or a combination thereof depending on stage.

Symptoms

- Abnormal vaginal bleeding (between periods or after intercourse)
- Foul-smelling or excessive vaginal discharge
- Pelvic or lower back pain
- Pain during sexual intercourse
- Unexplained weight loss and fatigue (advanced stages)
- Difficulty in urination or bowel movements (late stages)

Primary Causes

- Persistent HPV infection
- Early onset of sexual activity or multiple sexual partners
- Poor genital hygiene
- Smoking and tobacco exposure
- Weak immune system (HIV/AIDS, chronic illness)
- Long-term use of oral contraceptives
- Genetic or family history

Astrological Perspective

Cervical cancer is associated with imbalance or affliction of planets governing reproduction, hormones, immunity, and chronic disease. It often reflects long-standing karmic patterns combined with physical vulnerability indicated in the birth chart and activated during adverse planetary periods (Dasha).

Key Planets & Houses

- **Venus** – Female reproductive system, uterus, hormonal balance
- **Moon** – Immunity, fluids, hormonal rhythm, emotional health
- **Saturn** – Chronic disease, degeneration, long-term suffering
- **Rahu / Ketu** – Cancer, hidden toxins, karmic illness
- **6th House** – Disease and treatment
- **8th House** – Chronic, hidden, life-threatening illnesses
- **5th House** – Reproductive organs and fertility

Astrological Combinations Indicating Susceptibility

- Rahu, Ketu, or Saturn placed in or aspecting the **8th house**
- Severe affliction of **Venus** by malefic planets
- Rahu or Saturn influencing the **6th house**
- Weak or afflicted **Moon** indicating poor immunity
- Disease onset during Dasha/Antardasha of Venus, Rahu, Saturn, or Moon

Astrological Remedies

(Supportive in nature; not a substitute for medical treatment)

Mantras

- **Venus Shanti Mantra**
  Om Dram Dreem Droum Sah Shukraya Namah
- **Rahu Shanti Mantra**
  Om Bhram Bhreem Bhroum Sah Rahave Namah
- **Mahamrityunjaya Mantra** (108 times daily)

Spiritual Practices

- Abhishek of Shiva Lingam with water and Bel leaves on Mondays
- Donation of white clothes, rice, or sweets on Fridays
- Service or charity for cancer patients
- Regular meditation for emotional stability

Gemstone Remedies (after proper horoscope analysis)

- **Venus** – Opal or Diamond (only if Venus is benefic)
- **Moon** – Pearl for hormonal and emotional balance
- **Rahu** – Hessonite (Gomed) if Rahu is supportive

Gemstones must be prescribed only after full chart analysis.

Yogic & Ayurvedic Support

Yoga & Pranayama

- Bhujangasana – Improves pelvic circulation
- Ardha Matsyendrasana – Activates reproductive organs
- Anulom-Vilom – Hormonal balance and immunity
- Gentle meditation for mental strength

Ayurvedic Support (Complementary)

- Ashwagandha – Immunity and vitality

- Giloy (Guduchi) – Immune modulation
- Turmeric (Curcumin) – Anti-inflammatory support
- Kanchanar Guggulu – Traditionally used for glandular growths
- Triphala – Detoxification

(Use only under qualified Ayurvedic supervision.)

Dietary Recommendations

- Increase intake of green vegetables, broccoli, garlic
- Include turmeric, amla, and tulsi regularly
- Avoid processed foods, excess sugar, and alcohol
- Stay well-hydrated
- Prefer freshly cooked, sattvic food

Chapter Insight

Cervical cancer reflects a deep interaction between immunity, hormonal balance, and karmic patterns. While modern medicine addresses the physical disease, astrology, yoga, and Ayurveda help strengthen emotional resilience, immunity, and inner balance. True healing emerges when **medical discipline and spiritual alignment work together**.